THE WISH

THE WISH

The 99 things we think
we want most

Bill Griffin

CONSTABLE

CONSTABLE

First published in Great Britain in 2017 by Constable

1 3 5 7 9 10 8 6 4 2

A CIP catalogue record for this book
is available from the British Library.

ISBN: 978-1-47212-616-0 (hardback)

Typeset in Bergamo Std by D.R. ink
Internal design by D.R. ink

Printed and bound in Great Britain by CPI Group (UK) Ltd, Croydon, CR0 4YY

Papers used by Constable are from well-managed forests and other responsible sources.

MIX
Paper from
responsible sources
FSC® C104740
www.fsc.org

Constable
An imprint of
Little, Brown Book Group
Carmelite House
50 Victoria Embankment
London EC4Y 0DZ

An Hachette UK Company
www.hachette.co.uk

www.littlebrown.co.uk

For Minna, Eliza and Wu-Tang,
with love always and forever.

CONTENTS

'I wish I was a little bit taller,
I wish I was a baller.'

Skee-Lo

INTRODUCTION

About a thousand days ago I launched an app called 'Crowdwish'.

It's based on the – not particularly original – observation that everyone on earth has hopes, dreams and aspirations for their future.

These can be anything – from a sold-out Topshop dress to peace in Syria, from a rare book to a free school in a local area.

So I wondered whether or not there might be a benefit in creating a space for people to share their wishes, and created an app to do exactly that.

Crowdwish asks people to submit the three things they most want in the world and then does something In Real Life about the most popular wish, every twenty-four hours.

People's wishes have poured in from all over the world: happy, ridiculous, melancholic, funny and heartbreaking. Interestingly, the wishes are, in the main, ordinary everyday things, rather than annoying whimsies about being able to fly or spending the night with Ryan Gosling or whoever.

They are practical, close to home, easy to relate to, not inaccessible or absurdly over-ambitious – people wish they could communicate better with their parents, find a great pie, summon up the courage to confront their boss or discover somewhere amazing for a dirty weekend. That kind of stuff.

This book looks at ninety-nine of the most popular wishes and examines how to get closer to fulfilling them.

Pick the wish that most resonates with you, email us and we'll help you out in the way described. Somewhat meanly, you can only apply once. Harsh, we know. Sorry.

The email address for this is always the same: help@crowdwish.com.

1

'I WISH I WAS A MILLIONAIRE'

Of course you do, dear.

The best way to a million pounds is to start your own company, which is easier and cheaper, arguably, than ever before.

Here's how:

1. Find a solution to a real problem. Ideally one of which you have first-hand experience. Many shrewd businesses start by critically appraising something lame: a service which doesn't quite function as well as it should, or seems clunky or old-fashioned.
2. Build something a hundred people completely love rather than a thousand people think is kind of OK.
3. Don't mistake people saying 'Um, that sounds cool, I guess' as validation. That's just your friend being kind. Sorry.
4. Be conscious of the Pareto Principle: 80 per cent of meaningful results will come from 20 per cent of your time/endeavours. Find out what that means for you.
5. Turns out Yoda was right all along. Do, or do not. There is no try. Never talk about what you're going to do. It's meaningless. Talk about what you're doing right now. Today.
6. Seek mentors. Try and find someone who's been there and done that and believes in your vision, then use them as a sounding board.
7. Welcome problems and failures as chances to make yourself more robust. Never be downhearted or feel sorry for yourself. 'What does not kill me makes me stronger', as Friedrich Nietzsche once muttered to himself after another frustrating eighteen-hour day attempting to gain traction for his start-up (an app which empties human existence of meaning, purpose, comprehensible truth and essential value).

You can achieve absolutely anything, regardless of your age or background; like Bill Gates once said: 'If you're born poor, it's not your mistake. But if you die poor, it is your mistake.' Easy for you to say, Bill, what with your $80 billion and everything. God, man, have a bit of empathy for us little people.

If you're still stuck despite our sagacity, email us and we'll send you an idea for a business which, if executed properly, has the capacity to turn over £5 million-plus in the next three years.

Likelihood of this wish delivering happiness should it manifest: Pretty good probably, but not because you've now got two Range Rovers and a ski chalet in Courchevel 1850. True happiness comes from building something worthwhile that benefits others; so aim for that with your business ideas and see the money as a side benefit. Sorry if that sounds a bit preachy.

2

'I WISH MY HANGOVER WOULD GO AWAY'

'I sat up in bed with that rather unpleasant feeling you get sometimes that you're going to die in about five minutes,' said Bertie Wooster of hangovers. He was right. A proper hangover is truly awful.

As everyone knows, alcohol is a diuretic. This means it removes fluids from the body so, very tediously, drinking too much always leads to dehydration, which is what causes many of a hangover's symptoms.

Here's how to minimise your hangover the next time you go out:

* Line your stomach with something robust to eat before you leave the house. Everyone knows this but no one bothers doing it. It does actually make a big difference.

* Drink loads of water through the evening, if you can remember so to do. Yawn.

* Avoid mixing your drinks and, while this is a bit of a kill-joy style recommendation, don't completely tear up the dance floor – science tells us if you completely exhaust yourself, you'll end up getting even more dehydrated and depleting your energy levels much faster.

* The following day, try and avoid drinking coffee as it is another diuretic. Sprite is good – a Chinese study looking at fifty-seven different beverages found the lemon and lime drink helped process the alcohol out of your system quicker, speeding your recovery.

* Lots of people swear by a banana smoothie or milkshake, and a full English breakfast will give you an energy boost as eggs and meat are rich in amino acids.

* Exercise – if you can face it – is a reliable way to get over a hangover. But then so is sleep, which is much easier and infinitely more enjoyable.

Drinking alcohol is like borrowing fun from tomorrow, as someone once said. Sad really, that our bodies should punish us just for having a good time. Very Scottish Presbyterian.

Email us and we'll send you a little kit to help you get through the day the next time you're feeling hungover and pathetic.

Likelihood of this wish delivering happiness should it manifest: Fleeting though they may be, a bad hangover is a truly awful experience, so the upside of this wish is not to be underestimated.

3

'I WISH I COULD HAVE A
DIRTY WEEKEND'

Dirty weekends are expensive, self-indulgent, kind of sleazy and completely fantastic. Here's how to have the perfect one.

Agree to make it a ritual. Whether you're twenty-one or sixty-eight, married or just started dating, agree that as long as you're together, this will be something you will always do. That way you get short-term sexy stuff combined with a deeper feeling of security.

Don't stress out about it. These kinds of occasions can carry with them a degree of unwelcome angst. Will I be sexy enough? Will I sparkle over dinner? Will the whole thing be some kind of crushing disappointment? The key thing is genuine intimacy, so let your lover know if you're feeling nervous and talk through your worries in advance. Then there's a good chance they can be left at home. Your worries that is, not your lover. That would be beyond inappropriate and rude.

Let yourself go. This is an opportunity to do things you've fantasised about, outside the realm of the everyday. Embrace that. This isn't about domesticity and talking about the children's 'slightly off' history teacher.

Counter-intuitive though it may seem, don't stay in bed the whole time. Sustaining that smouldering atmosphere for a full forty-eight hours without leaving the room is way harder than it maybe should be. So take a walk on the beach. Visit the gym. Go 'antiquing'. Is that a thing?

Use it as therapy. Pick your moment obviously, but this is a brilliant opportunity to reflect on the strengths and weaknesses in your relationship. It doesn't have to get heavy, and every weakness should be balanced with at least five fulsomely acknowledged strengths, but use the intimacy to your mutual emotional benefit.

Get the location right, although the hotel doesn't need to be incredibly flash; in some ways, a down-at-heel motel in the middle of nowhere is sexier than the obvious 'luxe' candidates, which can so often feel cloying and slightly naff. Pack light.

Email us your postcode and we'll send you a blindfold. Ooh. Saucy.

Likelihood of this wish delivering happiness should it manifest: Short term, pretty good. It's a chance to reconnect and momentarily shed responsibilities, leaving the routine of everyday life behind, which has a long-term benefit too.

4

'I WISH THEY MADE GENTLEMEN LIKE THEY USED TO'

Judging by the popularity of this wish, people feel it's borderline impossible to find a true gentleman these days. In the interests of clarity then, here are a few rules for the modern gentleman – he can get away with failing at a couple, but not more than four.

★ A gentleman should be able to dance. And cook. But neither activity should be conducted ostentatiously; as a gentleman, a certain understated elusiveness is your defining characteristic.

★ A gentleman should have nothing to do with social media and regards Twitter and Facebook as facile and pointless. Tinder should be seen as kind of tragic and Snapchat should just elicit a quizzical raised eyebrow. Even texting is not really appropriate.

★ A gentleman should be quite closed off emotionally; he should hold something back and a part of him should not be accessible to others. He doesn't gush, unburden himself, cry. He is emotionally attuned to the needs of others but retains an element of mystery. This is vital.

★ A gentleman should smell right. This should be a combination of your natural scent, cologne, cigarettes and something indefinable but perhaps faintly animal.

★ A gentleman should dress well but never talk about clothes. He should own fewer, more expensive items, well-worn and cared for but never obsessed over. Any form of infatuation with 'designer labels' is off limits. He never puts 'product' in his hair.

★ A gentleman's understated manners are critical – he has a firm handshake, he stands up when women leave the table, offers his seat to others, opens doors, RSVPs to invitations immediately, walks on the road side of the pavement.

★ A gentleman should not get into fights. If he is reluctantly drawn into a confrontation, it is important to fight clean and to emerge victorious and unscathed.

★ A gentleman should treat every woman with the same amount of respect and humanity that he does his mother – he doesn't objectify women, other than the one with whom he is in a relationship. That can be appropriate under the right circumstances.

If you know someone aspiring to be a true gentleman, then email us and we'll send them a monocle or some cologne or a horse or something.

Likelihood of this wish delivering happiness should it manifest: Not bad. It would be good to think that old-fashioned values are still alive, but don't forget the words of Hollywood legend Lana Turner – 'A gentleman is simply a patient wolf.'

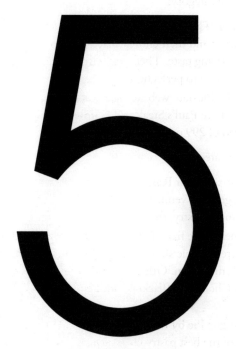

5

'I WISH I COULD FIND THE BEST
SLICE OF PIE IN THE WORLD'

This is the kind of wish anyone can achieve – easy, democratic and, more importantly, delicious. From Homer Simpson to Barack Obama, everyone loves a pie and, as Andy Warhol once said about Coca-Cola, it doesn't matter who you are; it's going to taste the same for everybody.

The title of 'Best Slice of Pie in the World' is always going to create heated debate so, after extensive research on both sides of the Atlantic, we've whittled it down to five contenders – two savoury pies and three sweet.

In the savoury pie category:

* The Ginger Pig. This is the 'poster child' butcher for the modern approach to meat and their entire operation revolves around animal welfare and amazing taste. Their pies – from beef bourguignon to pork and sage – are close to perfection.
* Paul's Pies. The Pie-rate website – dedicated to reviewing pies and nothing else – have Paul's Steak and Guinness pie in their number-one position, ahead of 299 others.

In the sweet pie category:

* Banana Cream and Pear Raspberry Pie from MissionPie in San Francisco. Legendary venue whose pies are characterised by three things: handmade pastry, fresh fruit and a focus on seasonality.
* Salted Caramel Apple from Four and Twenty Blackbirds in Brooklyn. This is an incredible pie shop, owned by twenty-something sisters Melissa and Emily Elsen. Other unconventional flavours include Green Chilli Chocolate, Blackcurrant Lemon Chiffon and Salty Honey.
* Lemon Meringue Pie by Laura Amos of the Dessert Deli in London. Amos is one of the best pastry chefs alive, has worked at the Ivy and Le Caprice, and supplies Fortnum & Mason and Whole Foods Market. Her Lemon Meringue Pie is beyond delicious.

So there you have it. The world's best pies. As an unexpected bonus, email us and we'll send you a list of the fifty best places for cake, pizza and tacos on both sides of the Atlantic.

Likelihood of this wish delivering happiness should it manifest: Short term, very good. All these pies are completely amazing. In the long term, obviously, obsessively craving any foodstuff is emotionally unhealthy and will only lead to a Henry VIII/Elvis Presley/John Candy-style demise.

6

'I WISH THAT PEOPLE WEREN'T SO ANNOYING ON SOCIAL MEDIA'

Here are the people we find most annoying on social media, which, it turns out, is basically everyone:

* People who post a picture of their friend, pulling an (un)funny face, accompanied by the caption 'Dinner with this one'. The phrase 'this one' is literally the most annoying thing in the world, attempting as it does to bestow some kind of legendary status on your probably perfectly nice but essentially anonymous dining companion.

* People who use the hashtag #blessed. Basically, this is a fig-leaf to legitimise shameless boasting under the pretence of gratitude. Also an attempt to invoke some kind of Eastern spirituality you'd like the world to think you're really into, which has 'being thankful each day' as its core principle. It's dying out now in fairness, thankfully.

* People who ceaselessly bleat on about how offensive they find Donald Trump. We get it. You're not a massive racist and you're super-engaged with the US political process. Well done. Top marks for emotional literacy.

* Likewise, all virtue signalling re disappointing EU referendum result. Yes, you wanted to Remain because you're totally modern and inclusive and stuff, but claiming 'I can't stop crying'? Really? You may as well just post, 'I would like to remind everyone I am really caring and sensitive. Like me, like me', and be done with it, frankly.

* People who post a photo of their Starbucks cup with their name slightly misspelled, frequently with the brilliantly original hashtag #Epicfail. Spare us.

* People who post the results of those incredibly lame Buzzfeed quizzes about that character you are from *Friends*. Great, you're 40 per cent Monica. That's wonderful.

* People who talk about something either 'winning' or 'breaking' the internet. People who say 'Wow. Just wow' or 'There are no words' or 'Mind. Blown' when posting a picture of something unremarkable. People who say 'Not a bad view from my desk today', when posting a picture of a beach from their holiday. People who call the internet 'The interwebs'.

If you're drowning in a lukewarm pool of social media vapidity, then email us and we'll send you a step-by-step guide as to how to get out. This is a metaphor by the way, albeit a convoluted one. There is no actual pool.

Likelihood of this wish delivering happiness should it manifest: High. Be especially wary of those who use social media purely to garner social approval; simple vanity clumsily disguised as selfless conviction.

7

'I WISH I WAS THE KIND OF
GODPARENT WHO BOUGHT REALLY
COOL PRESENTS'

Be not afraid, for here are the best thirty or so online stores in the world,* varying from really quite reasonable in price to insanely expensive. Most are at the former end, or at least somewhere in the middle.

'Labour & Wait' and 'Brookfarm General Store' are great for things for the home and kitchenware and stuff. As are 'Umbra' and 'Cachette', and 'OK' (okthestore.com).

'Manufactum' is amazing for sturdy, old-fashioned, beautifully made things from pencils to parkas. 'Field Notes' is completely perfect for pads, journals and planners. Also check 'Polite Company' for stationery and limited edition art.

'& Other Stories' and 'Opening Ceremony' are on point for women's clothing accessories, jewellery and bags. So is 'Free people' if you want a more California vibe or try 'Stylebop' for something slightly more luxurious.

Both Tate and the Victoria and Albert Museum have great online shops. As does MoMA in New York. '1st Dibs' and 'Counter Editions' are both beautiful if you've got cash to burn on art. For ceramics, 'Reiko Kaneko' is beautiful. The temples of Parisian chic 'Colette', 'Merci' and 'Chez Moi' all have superb online stores.

'Omero' is worth checking out for vintage and *brocante* style one-offs for the home. 'Mouth' is perfect for people who love their food. 'Ahalife' is like a huge, very well-curated flea market. 'Farfetch' is 400 deeply stylish boutiques all in one place. 'Goodhood' and 'Not Just a Label' are also pretty easy to fall in love with.

'Dude I Want That' and 'Firebox' are best for adolescent boys or men having a midlife crisis. 'Lutyens & Rubinstein' is the most charming bookshop in London and puts together batches of handpicked books for special birthdays and events. Try 'Insound' for vinyl, or 'Boomkat' for house and electronica. 'A Quarter of . . .' is perfect for old-fashioned sweets.

If you need help finding the ideal present for someone, then email us some details about them and your approximate budget and we'll send you some tailor-made suggestions.

Likelihood of this wish delivering happiness should it manifest: Pretty good. A well-chosen gift brings equivalent pleasure to both giver and recipient.

* If a site is US-based and you're reading this in Europe, then familiarise yourself with the website 'Hop-Shop-Go', genuinely life-changing, despite the annoying name. It basically allows you to shop from any US store, sorts the shipping and negates the need for a US credit card.

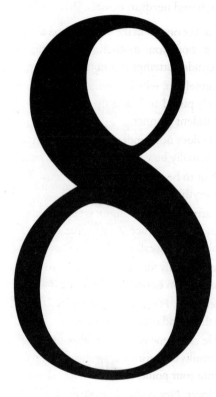

'I WISH I COULD FIND A
BOYFRIEND WHO WASN'T SUCH
A DOUCHE'

This was a super-popular wish, accompanied by numerous tales of woe, including one story in which a recently dumped boyfriend tattooed a big symbol of his ex's name on his stomach in order to try and win her back. It didn't work.

Here, in no particular order, are the ten principle characteristics any non-douchey boyfriend needs to possess. Preferably in spades.

1. Kind. He is never one to make you feel bad about yourself, or to be mean to or about your mother, or to be snappish with restaurant staff in a misguided attempt to impress you.
2. Funny. Genuinely so, which is not the same thing as getting inappropriately pissed and shoutily dominating dinner in a boorish and over-confident manner.
3. Equitable. He does not condescend or go on about how he thinks 'history will actually be very kind to David Cameron'. And so forth.
4. Generous. Not to be confused with ostentatiously insisting on paying for everything and expecting a blow job in return.
5. Emotionally articulate. But without being too in touch with his own feelings, in the style of Bruce Willis's character in *Friends* who couldn't stop crying about being called 'Chicken Boy' when he was six.
6. Grateful. He feels truly fortunate and lucky to be in a relationship with you, and you share an outlook on its future.
7. Properly interesting. He is capable of original thought without being in love with the sound of his own voice.
8. Receptive. He can argue with you without being annoying, resorting to insults or truisms, dragging up the past or deliberately misinterpreting your point.
9. Competent lover. Not endlessly making naff bedroom suggestions stolen from the pages of *GQ* or thrusting blindly for what seems like days.
10. Trustworthy. Only instinct and getting a sense of his past can really inform this.

You can maybe compromise on one or two of these, but no more. It may be helpful to tear this page out and refer to it ostentatiously during first dates.

Otherwise, email us with a brief description of your potential boyfriend and we'll tell you whether he's a keeper or not, using a completely subjective methodology all of our own.

Likelihood of this wish delivering happiness should it manifest: Substantial. We all need someone to love unconditionally and we all need someone unconditionally to love us.

9

'I WISH I COULD DO SOMETHING ABOUT MY AWFUL MOTHER-IN-LAW'

The bitchy and interfering mother-in-law is a familiar creation, much loved of old-school stand-up comedians and sitcom writers short on characterisation ideas.

In real life, if there are going to be issues, they will typically arise between a wife and her mother-in-law.

The wife feels the mother is controlling and interventional and appears to be in the grip of some kind of Lawrentian fixation towards her son, for which she urgently needs a course of therapy to which she would sadly never agree.

The mother-in-law thinks her precious boy is not being looked after sufficiently attentively, looks worryingly thin and that their children seem 'almost feral'.

The beleaguered husband appeals to both parties in a slightly ineffectual and hesitant fashion and usually ends up reduced in the eyes of both women.

It's all very English and awkward.

The difficult reality is that – despite the fact the mother-in-law in question may be overbearing, selfish and selectively deaf – she is still better treated with kindness.

As difficult as it may be to acknowledge, there is a very good chance the behaviour that appears to be so rude and narcissistic is driven by a feeling of fear and loss. Loss of her own family unit, subconscious jealousy of the new one created, anguish that her own experience and methods are now dated or obsolete, worry that she may not have much time left with her grandchildren, and hyper-sensitivity at being shut out, of being replaced.

Seen through a slightly more compassionate lens, the mother-in-law becomes someone to support rather than someone to flail against. Her motivations become less dubious, her seemingly thoughtless actions less pointed. Try that perspective for her next three visits, and if it doesn't work get in touch and we'll provide you with some tailored advice from someone who has navigated these choppy waters successfully.

Likelihood of this wish delivering happiness should it manifest: Well, as ridiculously clichéd as the archetype may be, the nightmare mother-in-law can be a huge source of marital tension and consequent unhappiness, so definitely a situation to sort, sharpish.

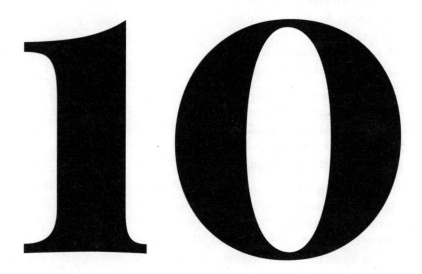

10

'I WISH I COULD BE FRIENDS
WITH MY EX'

The age-old question of whether or not to stay friends with your ex is one that divides opinion very sharply.

Despite the fact you may no longer be a couple, there's a person out there who knows you intimately, who cares about you deeply and with whom you have shared myriad experiences; someone connected to your friends and family, who understood your hopes and fears for the future, and with whom your entire life was shared.

Even if you're no longer romantically involved, it does seem strange that you would never speak to this person again; unless the relationship finished with some awful act of betrayal or in a way which was impossible to recover from emotionally.

But staying friends with an ex is easier if neither of you is in a fresh relationship. As soon as one party is part of a new couple, it becomes way trickier; not least because a bond with someone special from the past can, understandably, be seen as something of a threat to the intimacy you're now developing with someone new.

The situation is further complicated if one party is holding onto some residual romantic feeling or, more difficult still, a lingering hope that one day you may reconcile as a couple. Even if that dynamic isn't there, exes can still be territorial and possessive, and that can be very tricky for a new girlfriend or boyfriend.

It's worth asking why it's so important to you to stay friends in the first place and whether or not it's symptomatic of an absence of something in your new relationship. That may not be the case, but staying friends with an ex is very frequently one of those things, like going ice-skating or New Year's Eve, which sound great in theory but are often way more complicated in real life.

Anyway, if you're in a state of emotional imbalance about your ex – maybe you're casually stalking them on Instagram and they appear to be just a little too happy for your liking – then email us explaining the situation and we'll send you some tailored words of advice.

Likelihood of this wish delivering happiness should it manifest: It's complicated. Probably best to follow the wise words of Adele Dazeem:* 'Conceal, don't feel, don't let them know. Let it go, let it go, let it go, let it go' (repeat to fade).
* Google her.

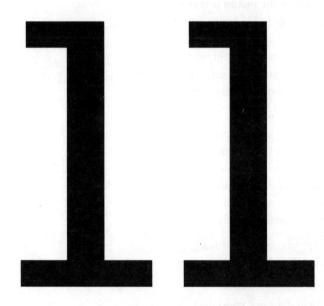

11

'I WISH I COULD ACCEPT MYSELF
FOR WHO I AM'

Self-acceptance is not the same as self-esteem. Self-esteem means the extent to which we are able to 'like' and value ourselves, whereas self-acceptance – arguably a more valuable but elusive quality – means embracing and understanding ourselves holistically, i.e. all our facets and qualities, not just the overtly positive or esteem-worthy ones.

This means facing up to, not denying, the parts of us that – up until now – may have been denied or ignored. This is hard, as they are likely to be the less attractive parts of ourselves – what some psychologists would call our shadow self – that which is covert, illicit, self-sabotaging, jealous or vindictive.

The truth of the matter is that everyone on earth has these traits and the longer we individually deny them then the further we will remain from full self-acceptance and the more these aspects of our personality will undermine our progress. In the most extreme cases, this can lead to a total dissonance between who we are and who we perceive ourselves to be, an emotionally damaging zone in which to live; and one that can manifest itself in many different ways, none of them healthy.

So to achieve self-acceptance requires the overt acknowledgement and acceptance of these characteristics. This is not the same as a complacent capitulation where those traits remain unchanged; it just means not denying they exist, loving yourself despite their presence and taking steps to overcome them; which is obviously impossible if their very existence cannot be fully recognised.

If you're struggling in this area, then acknowledge the parts of you that may be self-sabotaging. Write them down. Own them and take responsibility for them.

Accept and forgive yourself these characteristics; remember that everyone is a blend of that which we deem 'positive' and that which we deem 'negative', and we are all works in progress.

Self-acceptance means accepting the reality of a situation and our part within it, whether or not we find that reality palatable or pleasant. If we have the wrong beliefs hardwired into our minds, all the self-help books in the world will never make a scrap of difference.

Likelihood of this wish delivering happiness should it manifest: Potentially life-changing. If you're struggling with acceptance, then get in touch and we will send you something to help.

12

'I WISH IT WASN'T SO EXPENSIVE TO GO TO THE MOVIES'

Totally. Especially if you take children. By the time you've bought popcorn and drinks, a trip to the cinema for a family of four now costs around the same as the average three-bedroom house.

It's insane and the many people who have made this wish have our every sympathy. Especially those of them who recently made the mistake of shelling out to see *Batman v Superman: Dawn of Justice*. They're the real victims here.

Anyway, here's a few ways to make a trip to the cinema slightly less ruinous financially.

Never buy Pic'n'Mix. It is always disappointing and all the sweets taste gross. Especially the 'fudge' and those things you always hope will be proper Smarties but aren't. They're rank. You know this but still you go back. Resist.

In fact, smuggle in your own sweets and water. Don't feel this is tight-fisted; it's straightforward pragmatism and the cinema cannot legally prevent it. Cinema seats themselves are only about 25 per cent overpriced, whereas the food concessions are more expensive than they should be by at least 50 per cent, minimum.

Avoid paying the premium for those faux-leather 'VIP' seats. They are so not worth it. Likewise, the extra-wide screens called dumbass things like Xtreme or whatever. They can take the price of a ticket dangerously close to the £20 mark. Crazy.

Little-known fact; if you look after someone who is blind, infirm, elderly or disabled and you like to take them to the cinema sometimes, then only one of you need pay. You can get details in terms of how this works by googling 'CEA Card'.

There are also lots of Saturday mornings 'Kidz Club'-style things out there, as well as those 'Unlimited' passes, which probably only make sense if you go to the cinema literally every night.

Likelihood of this wish delivering happiness should it manifest: Pretty good, so email us and we'll send you some jelly babies to enjoy next time you go.

13

'I WISH I COULD STICK TO MY RESOLUTIONS'

Sadly, most of the research reveals that making resolutions is actually a really non-productive way of trying to create change.

This is for a variety of reasons – we make too many resolutions at one time, we shy away from the work required to complete them, or our resolutions are too vaguely expressed and therefore easy to wriggle out of. It may just be there isn't sufficient downside in not achieving them, so we fall back into old habits with little perceived consequence.

The real problem, however, is that willpower is a finite resource in most of us, and also a pretty weak one. As a result, it is really easily depleted, which is why it's hard to stick to resolutions if we're tired or hungry. Our brains are flagging and willpower evaporates. It's completely natural and totally understandable.

Knowing this, you are much more likely to succeed in any goal if you can avoid temptation completely, rather than try to resist it – so steer clear of situations that trigger problematic desires; if there's ice cream in your freezer, your puny reserves of willpower will swiftly be depleted in the ongoing battle not to eat it. Those high in self-control wouldn't even walk down the aisle of the supermarket that sold it, let alone have it in the house.

So the way to develop willpower is to acknowledge the inherent weakness of the will, and find methods to outsmart it and ways to avoid that internal conflict in the first place.

In other words, don't put yourself in situations where you are going to need to use willpower because the temptations will generally prove themselves to be too strong.

We're not advocating people should never resolve to do anything they want to achieve; obviously – that would be ridiculous. We're just pointing out that willpower is inherently a very weak resource, and armed with that realisation you will, paradoxically, find it easier to accomplish your objectives.

That said, accountability can really help in developing willpower, so if you have something you want to achieve next year, email your goal to us and every quarter we'll send you a nagging email to check your progress.

Likelihood of this wish delivering happiness should it manifest: Good. Just try and steer clear of temptation in the first place, remembering the wise words of Mae West: 'I generally avoid temptation unless I can't resist it.'

14

'I WISH I WAS BETTER ORGANISED'

Everybody feels like they're drowning sometimes. Fear not. Simply follow these three simple principles and unleash the productivity giant within. Or something.

Firstly, the best possible way to complete a job is to start it. The early twentieth-century Russian psychologist Bluma Zeigarnik produced a ton of evidence that once people began an assigned task, they would almost always see it through, even if interrupted. The reason is simple: things hang around in our heads if they're unfinished, just as once they're complete they tend to vanish. Our brains are hard-wired towards finishing tasks once they have been started, and shying away from ones we haven't yet begun. So get going and be honest with yourself when you are starting to procrastinate.

Secondly, know this: productivity is not about accomplishing a list of tasks. It's about achieving the most influential tasks; the ones that make the biggest difference in your life. The idea of trying to get everything done is actually detrimental to productivity as it tends to lead to feelings of stress, failure and rising panic. Relax. You just need to be really clear on the things that will most influence the ultimate outcome.

Thirdly, don't be paralysed by perfection – we're not advocating sloppiness, but 'done and in the world' is way, way better than 'perfect but still hypothetical'. Technology and collaborative working methods increasingly allow us to tweak things post their launch, usually influenced by the input of people whose opinions we care about, be they colleagues, customers or experts. Just get it done and stop making lame excuses, you lazy twat. Sorry, that was too much.

Anyway, however disorganised you may feel, we're here to help. Just email us and we'll send you a genius productivity technique that has the potential genuinely to change your life.

Likelihood of this wish delivering happiness should it manifest: Pretty good. If the practical issues with which we all have to deal threaten to overwhelm us, they contribute to a feeling of powerlessness and inadequacy, neither of which are healthy states of mind.

15

'I WISH I COULD DROP EVERYTHING AND TRAVEL THE WORLD'

This is the kind of wish that is more achievable than it first seems; the kind of thing we come up with reasons not to do.

Here are the most common, and their de-bunking counterarguments.

'I can't afford it'

The finances of a world trip are really the least worrying aspect – it can totally be done on a budget of £750 a month in places like the Far East, India and many parts of South America. Whenever travelling you will encounter people doing it for way less.

'Work won't let me'

If you are in a job you love and finding the requisite six months off is an issue, then you may be able to arrange a sabbatical. If you're in a job you dislike, then there's even less incentive to stay at home. This is the time to clear your mind and refresh your spirit.

'It could get lonely'

Don't worry about going alone. In fact, it's better. You will be truly free, properly in charge of your own itinerary and accountable to no one. You will meet and become friends with countless people, the majority of whom set out on their own too. It's how it's done.

'I'll miss my loved ones'

They'll be fine. Probably glad to see the back of you. Messaging apps and almost ubiquitous internet access mean it's easier than ever to stay in touch with those you love. Usually for free.

'I have young children and the eldest just started school'

Most local education authorities will be amenable to the idea providing you have a coherent plan for maintaining your child's education in your absence. This can be done in two or three hours a day, tops, so we are reliably informed. We know people with very, very small children who have managed round-the-world trips for a year or longer very successfully and the family have returned happy, bonded and inspired.

There are no reasons left now not to do it. Email us and we'll send you a page randomly torn from an old atlas to help choose your first destination.

Likelihood of this wish delivering happiness should it manifest: A trip around the world – either as a solo adventurer or as a young family – will make for an unforgettable experience and will provide clarity and inspiration. Do it.

16

'I WISH I COULD TELL SOMEONE MY SECRET'

This is a great wish. Secrets are amazingly powerful things: few conversations are more exhilarating than the ones that begin with something like, 'You have to promise me you are not going to repeat to anyone what I'm about to tell you . . .'

Keeping secrets can be stressful and emotionally corrosive. Hearing them can be thrilling or shattering. Revealing them makes us feel momentarily empowered, then often horribly guilty.

Everybody has secrets, but their universality doesn't diminish their power. In addition to our own, we also carry around other people's secrets, sometimes unwillingly.

Neuroscientists believe it's biologically preferable for people to reveal their secrets, and to try and avoid being confided in by others. Holding onto secrets forces the brain into a difficult, divergent position and can cause stress, anxiety or worse.

On a practical level, secrets create an artificial reality for those unaware of them, whose reaction when the truth is ultimately revealed is likely to be way more extreme than it might have otherwise been. As political scandals from Watergate onwards have shown, the original sin is usually way less damaging than the attempted cover-up designed to disguise it.

If you've got a story or secret you've never told a soul, but feel the need to get off your chest, then email it to us. While preserving your anonymity, obviously, we'll turn your secret into a postcard, put it up in a public place and send you a photograph, which you can quickly delete or bury in the deepest recesses of your hard drive.

Why? Catharsis – the act of making a secret public, even if anonymously – will relieve some of the bilious pressure that can build up if you're in possession of potentially devastating information.

Likelihood of this wish delivering happiness should it manifest: Higher than you might imagine. The scientific link between stress and the need to keep a secret is neurologically proven, so to respect your future self, difficult though it may be, you should probably refuse to hear the secret in the first place.

17

'I WISH I COULD FIND SOMETHING TO WATCH ON TV'

You so can. Especially with this whistle-stop tour of the best TV shows of the last five years. This list is definitive* and non-negotiable and no dispute will be entered into. Unforgivable absences notwithstanding, however, these seven shows are all life-affirming cultural events that can, without exaggeration, be described as properly unmissable.

* *True Detective*. A truly beautiful and terrifying vision of the Deep South, these eight episodes of completely gripping TV may very possibly be the best ever made. Genuinely. Sadly, season two is an embarrassing mess and should be avoided at all costs.

* *Community*. An incredibly accomplished and meta sitcom, which effortlessly subverts movies and other sitcoms to brilliant comedic effect. Among the cast – all fantastic – is a peerless Chevy Chase. Unpredictable, clever and hugely endearing.

* *Love*. Gillian Jacobs and Paul Rust star. She's a messed-up alcoholic, he's a goofy beta-male. Their relationship is a total car-crash, but the show is funny and very insightful and the characters both have a sweet vulnerability.

* *Stranger Things*. *Twin Peaks* meets *ET* meets *Close Encounters of the Third Kind* meets *The X-Files* meets *Stand by Me* meets *Super 8*. Trust us, you will love this. Brilliantly directed and quite scary.

* *Master of None*. Aziz Ansari stars as Dev, a jobbing actor who goes to auditions, tries to understand his parents and navigates the New York dating scene. That makes it sounds ordinary whereas the show is actually anything but, and has a genuinely new tone.

* *Silicon Valley*. Totally brilliant account of the ups and downs of a San Francisco tech start-up. Thomas Middleditch and T. J. Miller are outstanding and the show is hilarious.

* *Girls*. Lena Dunham's show is unassuming, engrossing and totally unflinching on the subject of female friendship. This is a properly insightful depiction of what it's like to have no clue as to what you'd like your life to be like. Spectacularly good.

So there you have it. Once you've got through those suggestions, email us and we'll send you a few more.

Likelihood of this wish delivering happiness should it manifest: Well, TV is rarely a transcendental experience, but that's OK. These are all a great way to spend a tired evening.

* Game of Thrones *isn't on there as we're too droolingly slow-witted to work out what's happening and* Breaking Bad *isn't on there as we've never seen it. Yes, we know; we're desperately uncool.*

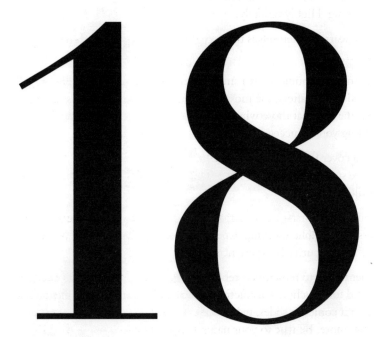

18

'I WISH I WAS BETTER AT PUBLIC SPEAKING'

Public speaking is frequently listed as one of the things people fear most. At the same time, it is one of the most confidence-enhancing skills to master, and one that may prove invaluable professionally. Here's how it can be mastered.

* One's fears about public speaking are usually irrational:
* You fear you don't really know your topic. You probably do.
* You worry everyone can tell how horribly nervous you're feeling. They really can't.
* You wonder if you'll stumble off the stage and everyone will die laughing. Highly unlikely.

These fears are themselves the very things that can inhibit a nervous speaker.

Whether your audience is a small internal meeting or a convention hall packed to the rafters, the most important thing is to take reassurance from the fact that those who have come to hear you will invariably be wanting you to succeed.

If you cover the main points and ensure they are made clearly, then you've succeeded. You are not a stand-up comic battling for laughs in a hostile club.

Even in the worst-case scenario, you have just succeeded in getting your worst-ever public speaking experience behind you. Ultimately the only cure for insecurity is experience.

Other things to remember: rehearse, rehearse, rehearse. Don't pace around too much; it's distracting for the audience. Maintain eye contact. When it comes to slides, pictures are always better than copy. Less is always more. Be true to your natural style, but check out both 'TED' and 'The Moth' for examples of good talks and storytelling.

If you've got an important presentation coming up, then email us a copy of your slides. We'll (gently) critique them and offer you some pointers.

Likelihood of this wish delivering happiness should it manifest: Maybe not 'happiness' in the conventional sense, but definitely job satisfaction. Even if your job doesn't call for you to present to people every day, it's good for underlying self-belief to know you can do so comfortably when called upon.

19

'I WISH MOBILE PHONES WEREN'T SO ADDICTIVE'

The thing about mobile phones is they are – slightly pathetically – highly compelling. They have become our umbilical link to the outside world: a constant companion with whom we check in at least 150 times a day, according to analysis undertaken by Silicon Valley venture capital firm, KPCB.

Maybe things have gone too far. 'Nomophobia' – the irrational fear of being without your phone – is apparently now a recognised psychological condition, while respondents in a recent survey said they felt so distressed and incomplete without their phone that neurologists found their loss evoked similar feelings to the 'phantom limb' syndrome suffered by amputees.

Many studies have found overuse of mobile devices has a highly negative effect on our relationships. Many of us have had the experience of being out with a group of friends, all of whom spend the evening not really talking to each other, wordlessly checking on other friends elsewhere. That, however, may just be down to my own very limited selection of anecdotes and inability to hold the attention of even the smallest group.

Are you worried you're spending too much time staring at your phone, swiping and prodding and jabbing like a maniac, snorting with laughter while your significant other stares at you askance, wondering what happened to the person they fell in love with from an earlier time, an analogue age of innocence? Possibly you haven't even noticed. But if you have and you want to change, then the best thing to do is determinedly schedule periods of the day when your phone is completely off – especially first and last thing. Gradually extend these periods to the point whereby it feels like your desire to stare endlessly at a tiny screen is starting to abate. Mealtimes are a good place to start. Holidays too.

It's holding back the waves, though. Next thing: embeddable technologies. Terrifying artificial intelligence. Internal headphones. GPS devices implanted under the skin. Contact lenses with inbuilt screens. It's a dystopian future and we're all headed there together, so buckle up, babies.

If you're concerned your phone is exerting a powerful and malignant influence over you, then email us and we'll send you a special sticker for the back of your phone, designed to drastically curb your mobile phone dependency.

Likelihood of this wish delivering happiness should it manifest: Probably quite high. The 'mindfulness' industry is constantly exhorting us to 'be in the moment' and phones are the enemy of that.

20

'I WISH I WASN'T IN THE THROES OF AN EXISTENTIAL CRISIS'

In simplest terms, an existential crisis is the acknowledgement that we're one day going to die – life is not going to go on forever and the days are numbered. Obviously, objectively we have always known this; the crisis comes from a visceral and abrupt realisation as to what it actually means.

It leads to the question, 'If I am going to die, what is the point of my life?' and our inability to answer this terrifying enquiry to our own satisfaction is the root of the crisis. You're not alone: according to a poll commissioned by the Open University in 2016, almost half of the British public have either had or are going through a 'life crisis' of some kind.

Existentialist philosophy puts emphasis on individual freedom and choice; it posits that we define our own meaning in life, and try to make rational decisions despite existing in an irrational universe.

In that sense the crisis cannot be ignored and in many ways it is your friend: asking yourself whether or not you are leading the most productive and fulfilling existence is not inherently a bad thing. It's our mind telling us that our accomplishments to date may not be sufficiently fulfilling in the time we have left. In some ways, it's just ambition manifesting itself.

Armed with that knowledge, the best way through the crisis is to raise your game – find something that has an inherently higher purpose, and to which you can make a contribution as part of a group. It doesn't need to be a full-time occupation, but it should have a special place in your affections and be something for which you are happy to make a substantial amount of time. Charitable work is one obvious example, or any project which will benefit others in some way. Email us a few details about yourself and we'll send you some tailored suggestions.

A midlife crisis is frequently accompanied by the soul-searching question 'Am I happy?', but the best way to become happy is to realise that finding happiness isn't the point of life. Finding purpose is.

Likelihood of this wish delivering happiness should it manifest: Major. Horrible cliché though it is, the years pass swiftly. Life is short. It is never too late to lead the life you were meant to, but it categorically will not fall into place of its own accord. It needs to be pursued single-mindedly.

21

'I WISH I COULD START MY OWN CLOTHING LINE'

Owning a clothing line is the kind of business that sounds great in theory. Creative, entrepreneurial, kind of cool.

The reality is sadly – like any business – more labour-intensive and dull. It's a hugely competitive market, with a lot of downward pressure on margin and a whole load of bear traps to fall into.

There are hundreds of things to get right, but two are arguably more important than everything else – the first of which is branding.

A brand is the intangible asset that delivers very tangible value. The brand is the thing that makes people pay over £2,000 for a handbag that probably costs less than £50 to manufacture. As they put it at Coca-Cola, 'If we were to lose all our production-related assets in a disaster, the company would survive. By contrast, if all consumers were to have a sudden lapse of memory and forget everything related to Coca-Cola, the company would go out of business.'

In other words, the brand is the thing that will make your clothing line stand out, and it's the thing people will pay a premium for. You have to nail the brand from the start.

The second key to success is to have a highly developed insight into your desired purchaser.

Just having a 'good idea' is not enough. What matters is having an acute understanding of who you think will want to buy your clothes, why and where it is you might successfully find them. This should be quite narrowly defined in the initial instance, as that which attempts to appeal broadly from the outset rarely does – things start in narrow channels. Start with a niche and expand from there.

Of course, there are myriad other elements that you would need to nail to create a flourishing clothing business: design, manufacture, distribution and marketing. It isn't easy but nothing worthwhile ever is. Email us and we'll send you a more in-depth guide as to how to get it right.

Likelihood of this wish delivering happiness should it manifest: Potentially double-edged. Managing your own flourishing business affords fantastic benefits, principal among them autonomy. At the same time, the potential for stress and possible financial ruin are never more than a trading season away. Sorry.

22

'I WISH I COULD QUIT SMOKING'

We understand the allure of cigarettes completely.

All the obvious downsides not withstanding – the insane cost, the horrible smell, the whole gruesome death thing – there is something seductive about cigarettes only smokers, and ex-smokers, appreciate. There must be or no one would do it, and in reality around a billion people do. It's not politically correct to acknowledge it, but smoking can be fun and strangely satisfying.

Smoking is not a rational thing, so using rational arguments against it don't fully work; it's a classic case of cognitive dissonance. A committed smoker can fully appreciate the health risks smoking poses, but that knowledge in and of itself isn't enough immediately to compel them to stop. How then to quit once and for all?

The thing to do is to change the habits that accompany smoking, which in turn will loosen the grip cigarettes exert.

One frequently overlooked factor is food and drink. Cigarettes are great after certain foods; especially things like steak and hamburgers. They are less satisfying after cheese, vegetables and fruit. Likewise, carbonated drinks, alcohol, tea and coffee all make cigarettes taste better. So many people find simply changing their food or drink (for example, switching from wine to a Bloody Mary) affects their need to reach for a cigarette.

Another thing is exercise: plenty of scientific research studies clearly demonstrate physical activity – even a five-minute walk or stretch – reduces the longing for a cigarette and may help your brain produce anti-craving chemicals.

A final point is obvious: if you're really dedicated to giving up smoking then make non-smoking friends. If you're at a party or club, roll with the non-smokers. When you see the huddles on the pavement, driven outside by a small white tube they allow to force them into the rain, give thanks you are free of that compulsion.

If you'd like to try an alternative, email us and we'll send you one of those e-cigarette things.

Likelihood of this wish delivering happiness should it manifest: Enormous. While its pleasures are often shrilly and piously dismissed, smoking is increasingly seen as anti-social and weak-minded. More than that, the satisfaction to be gleaned by proving to yourself you are stronger than your former addiction is huge.

23

'I WISH I WAS A LITTLE BIT TALLER,
I WISH I WAS A BALLER'

This is a reference to the 1995 Skee-Lo hit 'I Wish', which earned him a Grammy nomination and was played endlessly on MTV, although it failed to break the top ten in either the UK or the US charts.

His record label Sunshine Entertainment took most of the song's profits and, despite its popularity, Skee-Lo didn't grow an inch, stubbornly remaining at a height of 1.73 metres. The song – his only hit of note – has lyrics atypical of the syrupy mid-nineties Californian hip-hop known as G-Funk, with Skee-Lo listing a variety of different things he wishes for. It was unusual at the time for hip-hop artists to reveal their insecurities around their physical appearance or relations with the opposite sex, which may account for the song's enduring popularity.

The first verse is as follows, with annotations in brackets:

'I wish I was little bit taller' (Skee-Lo's not happy with his height.)

'I wish I was a baller' (He'd like to be able to play basketball professionally and hit the big time.)

'I wish I had a girl who looked good' (Skee-Lo went on to marry a very pretty girl and they have two children.)

'I would call her' (Only courteous to do so. Don't make it sound like it's some massive favour, Skee-Lo. God, you can be such a douche sometimes.)

'I wish I had a rabbit in a hat with a bat' ('Rabbit in a hat' is a girl of dubious virtue, 'bat' is a reference to Bacardi – the bat on the bottle's label. He'd like a drink with a call girl, basically. He's more settled these days.)

'And a six four Impala' (A 1964 Chevy Impala, which is a car.)

If you feel the same way as Skee-Lo, then face facts: If you're not the right height for pro basketball, pick another sport. If you are the right height but don't have the talent, then, again, pick another sport. If you have the height and the talent, then welcome to the NBA. If you literally haven't got a clue what we're talking about then email us and we'll send you the song via iTunes.

Likelihood of this wish delivering happiness should it manifest: Medium. Statistics show an extra inch of height translates to an average of £800 more annual income – the six-foot man makes five grand more than his five-seven colleague. Were one to make it as a baller, the average NBA player salary is around £4 million annually.

24

'I WISH I COULD BE AN EXTRA IN *GAME OF THRONES*'

Everyone loves *Game of Thrones*. Well, not everyone, but the series is one of the most popular broadcaster HBO has ever produced and tens of millions of people have been captivated by the epic serial. It's now officially the most illegally downloaded show in history.

Accounting for its astonishing popularity is tricky, especially as – is this just us? – it can be extraordinarily difficult to follow, and becoming familiar with the sprawling cast requires laser-like focus. That notwithstanding, the show effortlessly appeals to a much broader audience than the traditional 'fantasy' one.

This is largely down to the amazing characterisation and the sophisticated back-story; meaning the show feels closer to an historical drama, echoing the dynastic European power struggles of sixteenth-century Europe. There's no doubt it's powerful stuff.

Anyway, to the wish. We spoke to the casting agency that coordinates all the extras for *Game of Thrones*, which principally shoots in Northern Ireland.

If you'd like to be an extra, email us and we'll explain how it works. One fairly major caveat, however: usually extras must be Northern Ireland residents. There are practical reasons for this; the nature of the filming schedule means extras may be summoned to set with relatively little notice, so it's simply not practical to have extras registered from other parts of the world.

People report the days are long and there is inevitably quite a bit of waiting around, but it is so exciting being on set in such close proximity to the Lannisters et al. that the experience is definitely worth it.

We appreciate those of you who aren't Northern Ireland residents may now have started to cry noisily with disappointment, so email us and we'll send you a mysterious *Game of Thrones* gift.

Likelihood of this wish delivering happiness should it manifest: Being an extra on *GoT* would make a great story but there is a high chance of not making the final edit. Not worth moving to Northern Ireland for, despite the region's many features.

25

'I WISH I COULD TIME TRAVEL'

Well you can't, dummy.

That said, the possibility of time having a non-linear nature is something that has been speculated for hundreds, probably thousands, of years.

Einstein posited the hypothetical existence of 'bridges' through time and space – sometimes called wormholes. Numerous physicists have taken up his thinking on the subject since then, including academic titans Stephen Hawking and Kip Thorne.

So there is a little – fairly muted – support for the idea of time travel in some branches of quantum mechanics, but it's probably unlikely, not least because no one from the future appears to have come back to visit us yet (although the result of googling 'Reopening of the South Fork Bridge after a flood' is quite cool).

So in the absence of real time travel, let's do this instead: write a letter to a future version of yourself.

You may want to use it to check you've achieved a particular goal, offer encouragement to your future self, set a deadline for confronting a difficult issue or conversation, help yourself to forgive, or add anything else you think you might find inspiring, motivating or helpful in the future.

Send us the letter via email, and include with it the exact date you would like to receive it, weeks, months or years from now, and an address where you are confident you will be reachable.

Obviously we will keep the contents completely confidential, but on the day you specify in the future, the letter will arrive in the mail, from you, via us.

We realise this isn't 'time travel', obviously, but receiving a letter from your past self is a one-off kind of experience, and knowing it is coming – holding you to account – may be more interesting or influential than you imagine.

Likelihood of this wish delivering happiness should it manifest: Unknown. Should it be possible, the implications of time travel are too great to bother speculating on, so just content yourself with reading the Ray Bradbury short story 'A Sound of Thunder'.

26

'I WISH I DIDN'T FEEL SO DEPRESSED'

At any one time, 10 per cent of the population will be experiencing depression. It has a devastating impact on people's lives – taking away their energy, self-assurance, sleep, professional confidence and, most acutely, their ability to experience happiness.

If you're seriously depressed, it's difficult to imagine anything positive happening in the future and that thought itself is enough to deepen the feeling of depression. Opinions vary as to the best way to deal with the condition, not least because depression obviously varies enormously in terms of its intensity and duration.

Some studies suggest anti-depressant medication is only effective 50 per cent of the time, and the half that see an improvement in their condition will see some form of relapse back into depression at some point, effectively reducing the efficacy level to 25 per cent. The side-effects of anti-depressants themselves can be extremely difficult to live with, and can include physical weakness and insomnia.

It will always be impossible to say a definitive 'cure' has been found for depression, but there are steps that can be taken to defeat its symptoms. Research indicates the following activities have anti-depressant properties and, collectively adopted, may be a really powerful arsenal in beating depression. They really make sense and are as follows:

1. If you're physically able to do so, then exercise for a minimum of an hour and a half each week. Fifteen or twenty minutes a day can make a real difference.
2. Make sure you have good exposure to natural light – this means around half an hour of sunlight each morning in the summer, and possibly using a light-box in the winter.
3. Try not to obsess over negative thoughts – instead of dwelling, start an activity; anything to distract yourself.
4. Don't cut yourself off from people. Be as sociable as you realistically can. Talk to people and seek therapy – either a specific type like CBT or just finding someone who will listen and not judge.
5. Get a decent night's sleep. Minimum seven hours.

The other thing that can really help is taking fish oil. Try to have an Omega 3 supplement every day, ideally with a multivitamin and vitamin C tablet. Email us and we'll send you some.

Likelihood of this wish delivering happiness should it manifest: Obviously very high. Depression frequently destroys the lives of those who try and live with it.

27

'I WISH I COULD MEET THE DALAI LAMA'

OK, listen up. First of all, you need to fly to Delhi, which is possible from most capital cities in the world.

Having got there, you need to reach a village called McLeod Ganj, which is a suburb just up the hill from a town called Dharamsala. This is where the Dalai Lama has lived since being exiled from his native Tibet in 1959. His government is actually based in a village nearby called Gangchen Kyishong.

You can reach the town by taking an extremely atmospheric and very affordable overnight train trip from Delhi.

Get off at Pathankot station and get a taxi to McLeod Ganj from there. Once you've found somewhere to stay – Pink House is nice apparently – you can focus on trying to meet His Holiness.

Private audiences will not be granted on the day – there was a time when people enjoyed informal, unscheduled meetings, but no longer. These days, requests must be made online a long way in advance and require a fair amount of detail about who you are and why you want to see him. The Dalai Lama usually welcomes guests three times a week, on Mondays, Wednesdays and Fridays.

Make sure he is actually around when you arrive, as he tends to travel around the region teaching and is also abroad a fair amount: you can find his schedule on his website.

The Dalai Lama's office is in the Tsuglagkhang Complex and once there it is worth dropping the name of anyone you have encountered along the way who has a connection to him or his staff. In the restaurants and cafés of Dharamsala, it's easier to meet someone like that than you might imagine, but you may need to return to the Tsuglagkhang office a few times over a period of several days.

Just so you are forewarned, your audience is likely to last less than twenty seconds – enough time to be blessed and possibly have a photo taken. So don't have any illusions you'll be sitting down for tea and putting the world to rights, because that ain't going to happen unless you're maybe Richard Gere, to use a strangely dated example of a celebrity Buddhist.

If you think you have no hope of ever making it out there, get in touch and we'll send you an envelope containing a life-changing piece of Buddhist wisdom.

Likelihood of this wish delivering happiness should it manifest: Whatever happens you will absolutely not regret travelling to this amazing part of the world. It is genuinely magical, astonishingly beautiful and easy to live on £20 a day or less.

28

'I WISH I COULD TAKE A ROAD TRIP'

Road trips have a special place in popular culture. From the rambling yet mesmeric diaries of Jack Kerouac to the acid-infused antics of Ken Kesey and his Merry Pranksters, road trips summon images of a wilder era, allowing us momentarily to become free, young, untrammelled by responsibility and way cooler than we actually are – 'Tramps like us, baby we were born to run', we tell ourselves – or to at least take a momentary break from studying for our accountancy exams.

Here's five of the best:

Cabot Trail, Canada

Almost 200 miles through the most stunning part of Nova Scotia. The best part is the northern section around the stunning Cape Breton Highlands National Park with its incredible wildlife, including eagles and black bears.

Garden Route, South Africa

One of the most beautiful parts of a beautiful country – amazing vineyards, incredible beaches, uncompromising mountains. Straightforward and accessible.

Route 66, California, USA

Possibly the most iconic and well-known road trip in the world. Since the highway was decommissioned, Route 66 no longer exists on modern maps, but you can broadly speaking follow the original route from Chicago, Illinois to Los Angeles, California. The 2,500-mile stretch provides a truly representative perspective on modern America.

Gobi Desert, Mongolia

For those with a passion for off-road driving, the Gobi Desert allows for mile after mile of nothingness. Simultaneously featureless yet beautiful, this is among the most remote regions on the planet; when you get tired of being behind the wheel, explore on camel back and spend your nights at a traditional Ger camp.

Outer Hebrides, Scotland

A single, twisting track for 150 miles, this is one of the finest trips in the British Isles. Unexpectedly white-sanded beaches, mountain passes, beautiful islands, picture-postcard castles and wonderful scenery at every winding turn.

Likelihood of this wish delivering happiness should it manifest: Strong. Road trips work whether you're young and carefree, married with children or newly retired. Email us for a guide to the totally perfect Californian driving holiday.

29

'I WISH I HAD THE POWERS OF DEDUCTION THAT SHERLOCK HOLMES POSSESSES'

0920 2315211204 0205 0718050120 2015 08012205 200805
010209120920090519 20080120 19050513 2015 03151305 1915
140120211801121225 2015 1908051812150311 081512130519
200805 040520050320092205 230815 0116160501180504 0914
1908151820 19201518090519 011404 06211212 120514072008
141522051219 0914 200805 192018011404 1301070126091405 190520
01 0315131605200920091514 061518 092019 18050104051819 2015
040503090405 200805 02051920 1908051812150311 081512130519
19201518090519 011404 09142209200504 190918 011820082118
0315140114 0415251205 2015 13011105 080919 152314 12091920
0119 23051212 080919 16180506051805140305 230119 061518 200805
010422051420211805 1506 200805 1916050311120504 02011404 0914
2308090308 01 2515211407 2315130114 1401130504 0805120514
192015140518 05131612152519 1908051812150311 081512130519 011404
0418 230120191514 2015 21140405181309140 5200805 05220912
1612011419 1506 080518 19200516060120080518 0718091305190225
18152512152020 200805 02051920 05160919150405 1506 200805 2022
190518090519 230119 1618150201021225 190518090519 05160919150405
200805 180509030805140201030 8 06011212 022120 20080525 23051805
011212 161805202025 192018151407 011425230125 0906 251521
030114 1915122205 20080919 160120080520090301121225 05011925
03150405 20080514 1301250205 251521 1309070820 151405 040125
0718010421012005 2015 1908051812150311 19 1205220512 08051805
19 081516091407 0914 200805 1305011420091305 200805 0609181920
160518191514 2015 0513010912 2119 200805 1915122120091514
2015 20080919 1721051920091514 23091212 18050305092205 01
1325192005180915211 9 07090620 0914 200805 13010912 081512130519
191512220504 0821140418050419 1506 132519200518090519
1908051812150311 0919 09142209200504 061518 01 16180922012005
0121040905140305 23092008 1721050514 2209032015180901 0106200518
200805 0218210305 1601182009140720151 4 03011905 23080120 07090620
040904 190805 16180519051420 080913 23092008 011404 011223012519
1805130513020518 23080514 251521 08012205 05120913091401200504
200805 0913161519190902120 5 2308012005220518 18051301091419
08152305220518 0913161815020102120 5 13211920 0205 200805
2018212008

03080114030519 1506 20080919 23091908 04051209220518091407 080116160914051919
190815211204 0920 1301140906051920 08090708 0914 02152008 200805 0215151119
011404 200805 01130126091407 020203 2022 190518090519 1908051812150311 0919 0114
091403180504090212250 1202018010320092205 03080118010320051 8 23092008 10211920 200805
1809070820 130924 1506 0914200512120907050140305 01181815070114030 5 011404 1520080518
2315181204120914051919

Studies have found that one in seven Americans has more than ten credit cards, and in the UK the average household debt stands at £54,000 – almost twice the level a decade ago, according to a report by the Centre for Social Justice.

More than 5,000 people are made homeless each year because of rent or mortgage debts.

If you're worried about money, our advice – for what it's worth – is to start saving in little achievable ways that don't impact your quality of life too dramatically and make you feel depressed. Here's our top ten. Yes, parts of this are very boring but you don't dazzle your way out of debt, dude, he said, rich in alliteration.

1. Switch utility suppliers. uswitch.com is a comprehensive comparison site and a good place to start.
2. Likewise mobile-phone operators. Deals can often be done if they think you're going to leave. (All telco businesses are obsessed with reducing what they call 'customer churn'.)
3. Ditch pay TV and get Freeview instead. Possibly supplemented by Netflix.
4. Don't go shopping for food while hungry and always make a list and stick to it. Old-hat advice but the psychology works.
5. Take a packed lunch to work. There is no geeky shame in this anymore. In fact, everyone's doing it. It's almost fashionable.
6. Unsubscribe from any 'Daily Deal' or 'Flash Sale' sites that tempt you with last-minute bargains.
7. Drive less, walk more.
8. You only need to buy a coffee and croissant every day to spend £1,500 a year. That's a big chunk of most overdrafts.
9. Rent out a spare room, if you have one, via Airbnb or Onefinestay, if you're upper middle class.
10. Quit smoking. Not meant piously, but it's £10 a pack now. £10. A pack. Around £3,500 annually for a twenty-a-day smoker.

If these kinds of achievable adjustments resonate with you, then email us and we'll send you fifty more.

Likelihood of this wish delivering happiness should it manifest: Significant. Being in serious debt is a nightmare. It robs you of choices, sleep and self-esteem. Fight it with all your being.

31

'I WISH I KNEW WHAT TO DO NOW'

OK, follow these instructions carefully.

Put down this book and go downstairs.

Make provision for any dependents with whom you may be cohabiting and explain you may be out for a little while.

Put on clothing appropriate for the time of year.

Find the nearest mainline railway station and buy a ticket for London's Euston station.

Board the train and use the journey to relax or sleep.

When you arrive at Euston, exit the station on the Euston Road side (A501).

Cross over the road and locate Upper Woburn Place (A4200).

Walk half a mile or so in a south-easterly direction until you reach Russell Square.

In the middle of the square is a large communal garden called, predictably enough, Russell Square Gardens.

Locate a tree in the garden called *Taxus baccata 'Fastigiata'* or Irish yew.

In front of the tree is a metal plaque explaining that said tree was planted in memory of T. S. Eliot.

On the reverse side of the plaque you will find a small magnetised box.

Inside the box you will find further instructions.

Follow them.

Likelihood of this wish delivering happiness should it manifest: Impossible to know unless you comply.

32

'I WISH I COULD FIND THE PERFECT
PAIR OF SKINNY BLACK TROUSERS'

Like finding an elegant winter coat, someone who doesn't talk all the way through *America's Next Top Model* or the ideal moisturiser for your skin type, tracking down the perfect pair of skinny black pants is critical, but never simple.

As with the ever reliable Little Black Dress, the right trousers will become a staple part of your wardrobe and a piece that you go back to season after season. This is because, if you've found the right pair, they will be versatile, timeless and easy to wear.

Depending on what aesthetic you're channelling, skinny black trousers can make you feel like Audrey Hepburn or Kate Moss – you can wear them with a crisp white shirt and courts to the office; tuck a simple tee into them and work with skate sneakers and a leather biker for off-duty chic; or go glam with a silk camisole top and some vertiginous high-heel sandals.

But first you'll actually need to buy a pair so – if you're feeling clueless – try these basic rules and you'll have this classic look wrapped up.

Skinny girls, go straight-legged and tight to accentuate curves. Full-length or cropped, the world is your fashion-obsessed oyster. Curvy girls should embrace the boot-cut and kick flare.

Short-legged girls, go high-waisted. This little tip tricks the eye into believing your pins are of supermodel proportions. Almost.

If you have a shorter torso, then try a style cut to fit on the hip to balance out the silhouette.

Whatever size and shape you are, always ensure your trousers actually fit. The last thing you want is a waistband that cuts into your sides or hems that drag on the ground. So, if you can be bothered, never underestimate the leg-lengthening properties of having your hems tailored to fall a couple of millimetres short of your heel height.

See? Easy. Now get shopping. Those on a budget should try high-street staples like Zara, French Connection and Whistles. Those with money to burn should shop at Joseph and Stella McCartney.

Or email us your size and, once a quarter, we'll pull a name out of the metaphorical hat to win a pair.

Likelihood of this wish delivering happiness should it manifest: Not bad. Skinny black trousers are a total staple and knowing you've bagged the ideal pair is one of those things in life that is strangely and disproportionately satisfying.

33

'I WISH I COULD DECLUTTER MY HOUSE'

Everyone likes the idea of a simple, uncluttered home. Most of us, however, fall some way short of that ideal and frequently find ourselves unnecessarily hoarding ancient boob tubes, mountains of old magazines, little china dogs and stuff.

The most difficult thing about decluttering is knowing how to start tackling the problem as the size of the task appears to be too overwhelming.

We appreciate that this sounds incredibly boring, but the best thing to do is to devote a small amount of time each day – say half an hour – to clearing one little section at a time. Start with a countertop, then a bedside cabinet, then a drawer. Relax about the rest of the place – just do a little at a time, room by room.

Pick up each item and ask, 'Does this bring me any pleasure?' If not, bin it. Or take it to the charity shop if you think someone else would like to clutter up their house with it. This methodology – such as it is – is the basis of the bestselling Marie Kondo book *The Life-changing Magic of Tidying*, so props to her.

Once you get into the swing of it, you will find your emotional attachment to things loosens and you can start to declutter more rapidly. Try this: every day, find ten items to throw away, ten items to donate to charity and ten items to be returned to their proper home. Maybe turn it into some kind of super-lame competition with your spouse before having a pillow fight together and laughing at the sheer joy of just being alive.

If you stick at it, it should only take about 300 years to get the whole house sorted. Only kidding; you'll be amazed how much can be achieved in a month. The key – like anything – is to get started.

Email us and we'll send you some black plastic sacks, in what must be a shoe-in for the most boring giveaway of all time.

Likelihood of this wish delivering happiness should it manifest: As shameful, suburban and doily-ish as it sounds, having an organised home is actually really satisfying.

34

'I WISH I COULD READ TWO REAL BOOKS A MONTH'

Maybe two a month is too much. Start with one a month. You can do that; it's like ten pages a day or something. Jesus. Lacking inspiration? Try one of these ten books, some of the most original and thought-provoking novels of the last few years:

★ *All Involved* by Ryan Gattis. Violent but extremely powerful novel about the six days of the 1992 Los Angeles riots.

★ *Stoner* by John Williams. A new bestseller over fifty years after its initial publication. The story of an academic whose life is full of disappointments.

★ *Gun Machine* by Warren Ellis. Hardboiled detective thriller with properly fleshed out characters.

★ *Sweetbitter* by Stephanie Danler. Coming-of-age and coming-to-New York story about the seductive pleasures of food, wine and cocaine.

★ *The Vegetarian* by Han Kang. A woman's nightmares drive her to take up vegetarianism to the dismay of her family. Then things get really weird.

★ *The Son* by Philipp Meyer. A story of moral courage and companionship in the American West.

★ *Lanzarote* by Michel Houellebecq. A chilling portrait of alienation and hedonism in a decaying world.

★ *Beautiful Ruins* by Jess Walter. Gorgeous, glamorous novel set in 1960s Italy and a contemporary Hollywood studio.

★ *May We Be Forgiven* by A. M. Homes. Lots of people were very impressed with what critics called this novel's 'narrative intensity'.

★ *Gone with the Mind* by Mark Leyner. The narrative is set entirely in a shopping mall's food court, but the landscape covered by this novel is almost limitless.

If you need a recommendation for a novel and none of the above seems appealing, then email us with the name of the last book you really loved and we'll send you a suggestion for a compelling new one.

Likelihood of this wish delivering happiness should it manifest: Reading stimulates the mind, obviously, and staying mentally engaged can slow the progress of Alzheimer's and dementia later in life. Plus, it looks sexy in a public place.

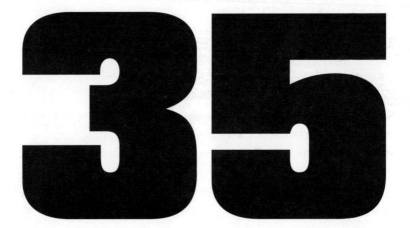

35

'I WISH THE COUNTRYSIDE WAS LITTER-FREE'

In the last twenty years, millions, maybe hundreds of millions, of pounds have been spent on various campaigns designed to discourage people from littering.

It hasn't really worked. People still drop rubbish in the street or throw litter from their cars and it's likely they always will.

Very few local councils regularly organise for litter to be picked up in rural areas, leading to a more acute problem than in urban areas. The absence of any local authority solution means a stark reality is staring us all in the face.

We need to pick up the trash ourselves.

Really sorry, but there it is.

You will have objections to this: you will mutter that someone else has selfishly cast aside a half-finished can of Cherry Coke, some baby wipes and a Wotsits bag, and why should you have to clean up after them?

You may feel concerned that if you start collecting rubbish, people may consider you eccentric and look at you with the kind of sympathetic curiosity usually reserved for those on day release. You may worry about your beautifully manicured hands becoming gnarled and dirty.

Sadly, these arguments are but trifles by comparison with the prize of returning the countryside to its natural beauty and the self-congratulatory and strangely satisfying glow you will bask in as you regard that now-pristine hedgerow.

If you like, email us and we'll send you a pair of rubber gloves so you can pick up some litter in your area.

It's like former PM Dave Cameron's one-time vision of 'The Big Society', which he only stopped talking about once a spin doctor told him no one had a clue what he was going on about.

Likelihood of this wish delivering happiness should it manifest: Pretty good.
Leave no trace, people.

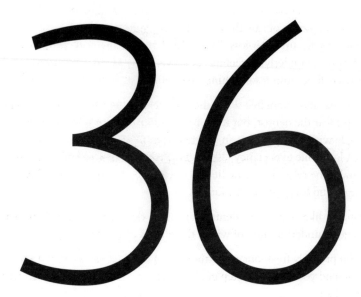

36

'I WISH I COULD GET OVER MY FEAR OF THE DENTIST'

An estimated 10 per cent of us have an exaggerated fear of going to the dentist; after spiders and heights, it is the third most common phobia.

Twice as many women as men have a dental phobia, but that's probably just a reflection of the fact women are generally better than men at expressing their fears.

There are a few different reasons why people get so worried about a trip to the dentist: they worry about the pain, they may have a bad association from childhood, or they're just uncomfortable with the lack of control and feeling of helplessness that comes with lying back in the dentist's chair.

Our fears are also exacerbated by the psychological dimension to our relationship with our teeth, which is acute and why stress dreams frequently feature their loss. Typically, these unconscious strings are indicative of underlying feelings of powerlessness or may mean we're worried about losing something, like a job or relationship.

So in real and intangible ways, there are legitimate reasons why so many people fear the dentist, but it is a really important fear to overcome. People with dental phobia may suffer from poorer health in general and even lower life expectancy. This is because poor oral health has been found to be related to some life-threatening conditions, such as heart disease and lung infections. Eek.

Happily, like all phobias, dental fear can be overcome, especially if there is a good understanding of where the phobia originated.

If you properly freak out at the thought of the dentist then email and we'll send you a step-by-step guide, which, if followed assiduously, will really help.

Likelihood of this wish delivering happiness should it manifest: Reasonable. It's not just about the dentist. Overcoming a fear in one area of their life frequently helps people achieve their potential in another.

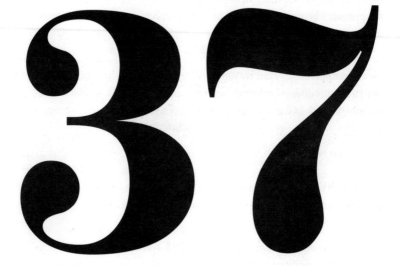

37

'I WISH I COULD FOLLOW MY PASSION'

The advice 'Follow your passion' is frequently and gleefully dispensed, as if encouraging people's greatest enthusiasms is a fail-safe path to career satisfaction and limitless riches.

It can easily be argued, however, that following your passion is actually an ill-advised, high-risk and immensely stressful path to take through life.

There are a few reasons for this.

Firstly, most people's passions don't lead to necessarily brilliant employment opportunities. A study of college students by the University of Quebec discovered 84 per cent of them had passions, and 90 per cent of these passions involved sports, music and art. Only 3 per cent of jobs, however, are in the sports, music and art industries. The obvious outcome of this is that jobs in these fields are fiercely contested with the majority of applicants being unsuccessful in their attempts to break into those industries.

Secondly, our passions and interests change more markedly over time than we often appreciate. That by which we are really enthused when we are in our late teens or early twenties will have evolved significantly by the time we hit the peak of our careers twenty or so years later.

Thirdly, again counter-intuitively, people tend to be very poor judges of that which will make them happy in the future. We tend to overestimate the intensity and duration of positive changes to our lives, which is why people will sometimes decide to pursue their dream of, say, working for a charity before discovering six months later that they're no happier than they were previously.

Finally, your own passion is secondary to that which makes businesses successful: the ability to anticipate and cater profitably to customers' needs. You may be passionate about hillwalking, but that doesn't mean opening a shop selling walking poles and rucksacks is the right decision.

So, strange as it may seem, when it comes to your career, maybe it's best not to follow your passion. Instead, the question when considering how best to use the 80,000 hours we work on average during our lifetimes is simple: 'Am I likely to be able to succeed more in this career than another one I am also considering?'

Likelihood of this wish delivering happiness should it manifest: Not as impactful as you would imagine. 'Following your passion' is a clichéd falsehood and an open invitation to making a mess of your life. Attempting to make money from your passion is a sure-fire way of killing the passion itself, somewhat paradoxically.

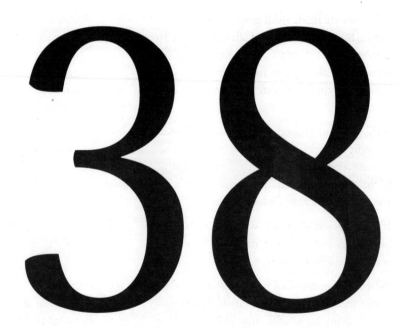

38

'I WISH I COULD LEARN ABOUT WINE'

Isn't this one of those things it's much better just to blag?

It can take many, many years and eye-watering sums of money truly to understand wine. More than that, it's maybe one of those subjects of which the more you know, the more of a bore you become.

Instead, just wing it. If you can muster sufficient authority and mock expertise, it's very rare you'll find someone to contradict you, especially as no one really listens when people start talking about wine anyway.

Here, then, is how to sound like a wine snob without actually knowing anything at all.

All wines are made from grapes. You knew that, right? Only some wines, however, are named after grapes – Chardonnay and Cabernet Sauvignon, for example. The majority – like Bordeaux or Rioja – are named after the regions from which they come. Even that incredibly prosaic insight can be carefully manipulated in the quest to sound educated.

Swill the wine around in the glass, sniff it and murmur you're worried it might be corked. This is where the cork has failed and the wine has become contaminated with a chemical known as TCA. Then take a sip of the wine and declare it 'fine, actually', which it invariably will be as less than 5 per cent of wines are corked.

If a wine is red, declare it smells like a berry. Any berry will do – blackberry and raspberry are probably best. If it's white, mutter something about lemons.

When all else fails, just make stuff up. No one will argue, they just might secretly think you're either slightly mad or very pompous. But if they're drinking heavily, any outlandish thing will probably sound fairly plausible.

Anyway, if you want to go down a more legitimate path towards one day becoming a Master of Wine – an accolade achieved by less than 350 people in the world currently – email us and we'll send you a little wine guide.

Likelihood of this wish delivering happiness should it manifest: Low. Possibly medium. Whatever.

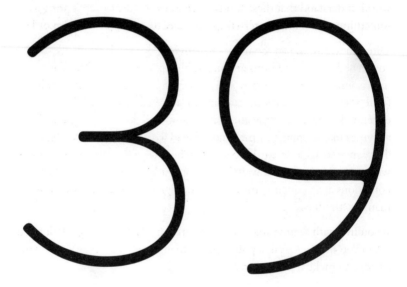

39

'I WISH PEOPLE UNDERSTOOD WHAT IT'S LIKE TO HAVE AN INVISIBLE ILLNESS'

Invisible illnesses are those defined as having little or no external manifestation – sufferers may appear 'fine', but in reality may be afflicted with any one of a number of conditions, all of which severely impede their ability to live a straightforward, 'normal' life.

These illnesses include things such as rheumatoid arthritis, migraines or back pain. Alternatively, the conditions may be neurological in nature like ME, fibromyalgia or chronic fatigue syndrome.

Because they have no outward manifestation, it is extremely easy for sufferers to be considered essentially well enough to function. As a consequence, it can be very difficult to have the condition taken seriously, receive appropriate care or disability benefits and have the world understand that these kinds of illnesses are just as debilitating as something with a clear external appearance, such as a broken arm or leg.

Often they can, in fact, be more challenging. For the individuals concerned these conditions are incredibly oppressive and frequently imprisoning, and steal energy and *joie de vivre*. Energy is an extremely finite resource that must be carefully measured and judiciously expended. Conserving the amount of stamina required for 'simple' activities like shopping or meeting a friend for a drink can take days. They may struggle to work, to attend school or college, or to socialise with others; even a short walk can become an enormous effort. The conditions are frequently misunderstood, ignored or just regarded by many as 'tiredness'.

If you live with an invisible illness and are frustrated at being overlooked when you need a seat in a public place, then email us and we'll send you a badge to make things clearer.

Likelihood of this wish delivering happiness should it manifest: Significant. It's horrible not having people acknowledge or realise the circumstances that may be negatively impacting you. Even a little understanding goes a really long way.

'I WISH I DIDN'T DOUBT MYSELF
SO MUCH'

In reality, no one thinks they're cool enough, pretty enough, clever enough or funny enough. From Wolfgang Amadeus Mozart to Paul John Gascoigne, the great geniuses in history have been plagued with self-doubt. Intelligent people have internal crises both large and small; confidence fluctuates, that is its nature. Nor is the myth true that we become more settled and full of self-belief as we get older, sadly.

Here are some things to try and get into the habit of doing a little more frequently than may initially feel natural. If you can succeed in these, slowly but very definitely your confidence levels will rise. We won't pretend it doesn't take work, like everything worthwhile, but try it.

★ Don't compare yourself to others. Other people's lives always appear to be way more sorted than they are in reality.

★ Slowly but determinedly detach from people who make you feel bad about yourself. There doesn't need to be a showdown, although sometimes a showdown can be cathartic. Like Mark Twain said, 'Keep away from people who try to belittle your ambitions. Small people always do that, but the really great ones make you feel you too can become great.'

★ Try and worry less about fitting in. The world's most respected people are mavericks and it takes an unreasonable man, or woman, to change the world. There's really no need for you to conform.

★ Say 'No' more. Be selective about the things you agree to do. This makes it easier to keep your word and the more you keep your word, the higher your self-worth will be.

★ Let go of grievances and things from the past that may be holding back your confidence. If you're struggling to get over a break-up, always remember the best revenge is a life well lived.

★ Eighty per cent of life is showing up. So show up. Make the call. Apply for the job. Speak your mind. Take the first step. Ignore the inner voice that makes you feel awkward or stupid or uninspiring. It lies. Take no shit from anybody.

Email us and we'll send you a little amulet to keep with you at all times to remind you to never lose faith in yourself.

Likelihood of this wish delivering happiness should it manifest: High. Confidence is persuasive, sexy, charming. You need to cultivate it or at least become adept at insouciantly faking it.

41

'I WISH I COULD CLIMB MOUNT KILIMANJARO'

You totally can. By all accounts it's an amazing experience; beautiful, challenging and uplifting in equal measure. It's also the kind of challenge most people can take on, although it does require some planning.

Here are five things you need to know about climbing the world's tallest freestanding mountain:

1. Fitness. You will be walking for around six or seven hours a day. Cardiovascular exercise is really important in advance, but you don't need to be an absurdly fit, ultra-marathon runner or anything. In fact, many people who are supremely fit get unstuck on the mountain as they ascend too quickly and don't give themselves time to acclimatise. You need stamina and determination in spades, though. These can be built up by some decent hillwalking in advance of your trip.

2. Altitude. By far the most common reason for abandoning an ascent is altitude sickness. This is best avoided by climbing slowly, taking a rest on the third day and keeping your fluids up. Listen to the advice of others and when in doubt gradually descend. Headaches and dizziness are the first signs that the altitude is having a bad effect on you.

3. Equipment. Get the right kit. You will need to be able to layer up. Thermals, mid fleece and good-quality outer jacket are completely vital. Likewise, decent climbing boots and gloves. A high-tog sleeping bag is another essential.

4. Food. You will be expending a large amount of energy. As a result, energy bars, biscuits and chocolate are totally indispensable, even though you may find your appetite is significantly less than usual.

5. Charity. One of the best and most popular ways to climb the mountain is to affiliate yourself with a charity that frequently supports people wanting to do the climb. They take care of everything for a low administration fee in exchange for an agreement that you will raise a certain amount for their cause. Google 'Kilimanjaro charity' for specifics.

If you're climbing Kilimanjaro for charity, then email us the link to your charity page and we'll sponsor you.

Likelihood of this wish delivering happiness should it manifest: As long as you're up to it, then good. It's a great achievement and will provide a fantastic memory, which will last a lifetime.

42

'I WISH I KNEW WHAT TO DO
ABOUT MY CHILD BEING BULLIED'

For those who have been through it, and those close to them, bullying is a truly horrendous thing to endure.

It's something a depressingly high number of children experience too – according to the UK's annual bullying survey almost half of young people experience bullying before the age of eighteen and a quarter of those bullied experience intimidation on a daily basis; 40 per cent have never told anyone they were being bullied; 30 per cent of victims go on to self-harm; almost 60 per cent said bullying impacted on their studies; 160,000 children in America stay at home every day because of bullying.

The emotional legacy of bullying can last a lifetime, with many middle-aged adults effortlessly able to recall the name of the person who humiliated them back in school.

It is agonising for parents, who are likely to feel angered and outraged about any kind of threat to their children's well-being, especially in a place that is responsible for their care. As a result, it is really easy for parents to fly off the handle themselves and react emotively to the news their child is being victimised or intimidated. Unwittingly, this creates the worst possible context for a child to open up and discuss the issue, making it less likely they will talk about the problem if it continues.

However difficult it may be, staying calm, level and responsible will make you way better equipped to deal with the situation in a rational and coherent way, which is exactly what your child needs to see in this situation – otherwise, they are effectively being left to deal with the problem themselves.

So, however strong the impulse may be, avoid the temptation of rushing in and yelling at the perpetrator or challenging their father to a bout of bare-knuckle boxing in the playground.

If your child is a victim of bullying, email us and we'll send them a little present to help them stay strong.

Likelihood of this wish delivering happiness should it manifest: Significant. The thought of someone being unpleasant to one's child is awful. Being able to master the situation is totally crucial.

43

'I WISH I COULD ADOPT A
BABY PUG'

If you're seriously thinking about adopting a pug, then here are ten things you need to know.

1. Pugs are considered the oldest breed of dogs and were originally bred to sit on the laps of Chinese emperors. As a consequence, they tend to carry themselves with a kind of regal dignity, but manage to combine it with being incredibly affectionate, playful and outgoing.

2. Pugs are companion animals and they want to be with their humans whenever possible. Despite their occasionally grumpy faces, they adore people and will follow their owners everywhere.

3. This makes them ideal pets for children, but pugs are also brilliant for elderly people, as they don't require much exercise.

4. Pugs are clever in their way, but have zero sense of direction and are absolutely not the kind of dogs that can easily find their way home if lost.

5. Pugs need protecting around water as their broad heavy chests mean they don't tend to be brilliant swimmers.

6. In fact, they need a watchful eye at all times as pugs are – scarily – the most commonly abducted breed of dog.

7. Pugs are short-haired, obviously, but shed hairs every day. So they're not ideal for stressy types who care about that kind of thing.

8. As they get older, pugs snore more frequently when they're sleeping, and may be susceptible to respiratory problems.

9. Celebrities adore pugs. Their list of famous owners is way too long to even start writing down, but includes George Clooney. And Queen Victoria. And Jessica Alba. And every other celebrity in the world.

10. A group of pugs is called a 'grumble', which is literally the sweetest thing in the world.

If you really think you might adopt a pug, then email us. We'll send you a file in the post containing everything you need to know.

Likelihood of this wish delivering happiness should it manifest: Good. Dogs are better than people, many believe. They are always happy, learn faster and can get away with licking strangers.

44

'I WISH I COULD FIND MY SOULMATE'

Finding your soulmate isn't easy. Like a lot of quests, it can, in fact, be a nightmare.

It's so fraught it's a wonder anyone bothers dating at all, when they could be home alone watching *Homes under the Hammer* and eating dim sum in their pyjamas, which is obviously preferable to sitting opposite a stranger in Pizza Express and asking them how many siblings they have.

In one sense the explosion in online dating offers greater choice than ever; on the other hand there's the argument apps like Tinder make embryonic relationships too casual and disposable and therefore less likely to culminate in the ultimate goal of finding someone with whom you can imagine growing old.

OK, here's the deal. Let us help you find that person with whom you are going to have a feeling of deep and natural affinity. If you're looking for your soulmate, just email us with the following information:

★ Your age, gender, location
★ What you're looking for in a soulmate
★ What you're better at than 90 per cent of the population
★ The last book you read
★ One deal breaker, i.e. something you would be unable to tolerate in a potential boyfriend or girlfriend

We will look over the various submissions and see if there are any obvious pairings.

Then we will, obviously completely anonymously, email your answers to the person who we think you might get on with, and email you with theirs.

If you both agree you'd like to meet, we will introduce you over email and a lifetime of happiness can begin. It's brilliant, it's simple, it's free and it can't fail.

When you get married, you don't have to thank us in the speeches, but it would be a bit strange if you didn't.

Likelihood of this wish delivering happiness should it manifest: Middling. A soulmate is someone you can trust with absolutely anything and everyone needs one of those.

45

'I WISH I COULD COME TO TERMS
WITH THE DEATH OF SOMEONE
I LOVED VERY MUCH'

Grief is a deeply strange and bewildering thing.

We can readily recall our previous – less complicated – existence yet it is suddenly reduced to a distant memory as the world around us becomes immeasurably different in a single instant.

One of suffering's strangest aspects is how, while our inner turmoil roils and rages, external things continue in their usual way; how acute suffering happens 'while someone else is eating or opening a window or just walking dully along', as W. H. Auden described it.

The famous five stages of grief – denial, anger, bargaining, depression and acceptance – are maybe a passable framework for understanding what is happening to us, but the grieving process is not akin to travelling down a railway line, stopping at a neat succession of stations. It's infinitely more complicated and messy than that. C. S. Lewis, in his book *A Grief Observed*, writing about the death of his wife, says:

> *No one ever told me that grief felt so like fear. I am not afraid, but the sensation is like being afraid. The same fluttering in the stomach, the same restlessness, the yawning, I keep on swallowing. At other times it feels like being mildly drunk or concussed. There is a sort of invisible blanket between the world and me. I find it hard to take in what anyone says . . . Yet I want the others to be about me.*

Grief takes away faith, steals sleep, our ability to function and frequently destroys relationships. We are ultimately alone with it, adrift in the storm, intermittently sighting land before being dragged under once more.

And maybe therein lies the answer, in as much as there is one. In the same way we exhaust ourselves swimming against the current or attempting to defeat those forces that will forever be too strong for us, we should surrender to those feelings, accepting in time that their power will diminish, while knowing in ways both significant and inconsequential that we will never be the same again.

If you've recently suffered a bereavement, get in touch and we'll send you a brilliant essay, which we really hope will help.

Likelihood of this wish delivering happiness should it manifest: Inherently strong. No two individuals grieve in the same way but everyone benefits from accepting help when it is offered and talking to others.

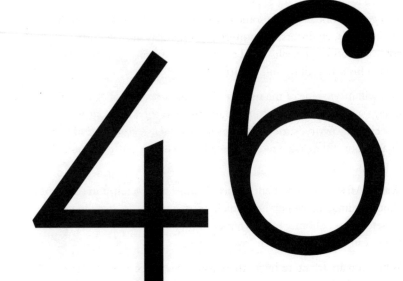

46

'I WISH I COULD TAKE A
HUMANITARIAN TRIP TO AFRICA'

This isn't something you can do on a whim. It's a project to which you need to commit, perhaps more than any career. It is not a soft option for people looking to 'find themselves'.

According to a field worker (who has worked in the Balkans, Israel and the occupied Palestinian territories, in Afghanistan and throughout Africa) and borne witness to things most of us will never see, let alone actively look to alleviate, here's what you need to know.

You are going to visit places where you would never go as a tourist or on holiday. Inaccessible, remote places. This is an extraordinary opportunity on some levels but also means rough living: lack of access to water, questionable food, risk of catching something nasty (typhoid, cholera, etc.).

You get to work alongside some of the most talented lawyers, health professionals, engineers, economists, agronomists, nutritionists, communications specialists and telecommunications experts in their field. This is humbling and inspiring.

You will meet some of the most resilient and remarkable people alive today – children, the elderly, men and women alike – who have, especially in Africa, suffered as a result of violent conflict and natural disaster but still manage to emerge upbeat, smiling and with the will to go on.

War in Africa – as elsewhere in the world – tends to result in some almost unimaginable horrors, which we struggle to envisage in our cosseted lives at home. It is extremely difficult to prepare for this and, again, can be very difficult to recover from.

While you are trying to help others your own life may be at risk – increasingly, humanitarian workers are not just in danger of being caught in the crossfire of conflict but are themselves a direct target for theft, kidnap and murder.

If you would like to meet up for a serious conversation with someone who has direct experience of working for a non–governmental organisation (NGO), please email us and we can facilitate it.

Likelihood of this wish delivering happiness should it manifest: It takes more than a kind heart to make a good humanitarian aid worker. Before you take the next step, just be sure you have the right skills to offer and you're prepared to deal with the suffering you will have to address face-to-face, day after day.

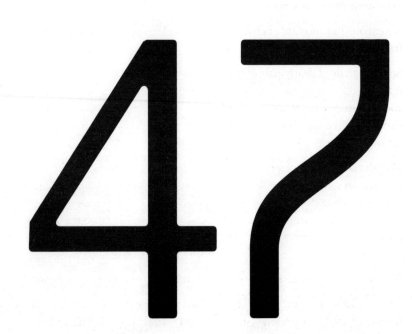

47

'I WISH I WASN'T SUCH A
CONTROL FREAK'

If you suspect that you are too controlling, it's because you probably are.

At least you're worried about it; lots of controlling people don't recognise the trait in themselves and are unaware of the impact their controlling behaviour has on others, that is to say, an incredibly annoying one.

Controlling people tend to visualise the future way too exactly and have a specific set of expectations for every event, conversation and random Sunday brunch. Inevitably life has other ideas and their idealised vision so differs from reality that they find themselves in the grip of some kind of hysterical over-reaction.

It's exhausting and futile behaviour that drives people away and is deeply frustrating to be around.

So what to do? Clearly part of this is about learning to let go, and realising the people you have around you are as competent, intelligent and industrious as you are. Probably more so, and less irritating. Sorry, that was a bit mean, but controlling behaviour is totally ego driven, so get over yourself.

Like the acquisition of any new skill, learning to relax properly takes practice, so start with one small area of your life and apply your evident steely determination to being super-chilled about it. Most happiness stems from the mismanagement of your own expectations, so try to avoid creating a perfect picture in your mind as to what things are meant to be like.

So maybe let someone else book dinner and resist calling in advance to ask thousands of questions about sustainability and food miles.

Or if on holiday with friends, try and avoid scrutinising the villa online in advance. When you get there, don't wake people up every morning by insisting they accompany you on some tedious excursion to some tedious cathedral you've read about.

Or possibly delegate responsibility for a project at work without shrieking instructions to your poor underlings. Or take a walk without a set destination. Or let someone else map read. Or don't criticise anyone or anything for twenty-four hours.

If you struggle with control issues, then email us and we'll send you something to help.

Likelihood of this wish delivering happiness should it manifest: More than you might be comfortable acknowledging. They might be scared to tell you to your face, but secretly people think you're a right pain in the ass.

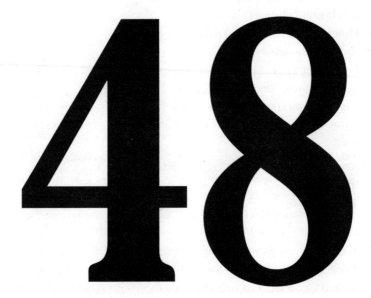

48

'I WISH CAKE MADE EVERYTHING BETTER'

Totally. That would be amazing. Sadly, life tends to be a bit more emotionally complex than that. Sorry.

Instead here, in reverse order, are the best cakes in the world, ranked purely subjectively by us. Doubtless you will disagree and we're sorry about that, too. What is indisputably delicious, however, is our secret and definitive recipe for the ultimate chocolate cake, which we will gladly share with you if you'd like to email us.

Anyway, to our chart of cakes, based solely on a random poll of the fattest people we know.

10. Any birthday cake when you're six or under. Cake will never be as good again, whatever the recipe.
9. Dundee cake. It is kind of delicious sometimes. Doesn't need the almonds, though.
8. Lemon drizzle. Consistently amazing, even if the texture can be disconcertingly 'damp' on occasion.
7. Classic Victoria sponge. Summery perfection. That sounded really camp, but it is a very worthy entrant if eaten still warm from the oven.
6. Those Colin the Caterpillar ones from Marks & Spencer. Tacky genius and the staple of slightly awkward 'cake and stare' office celebrations everywhere.
5. 'Almond Honey Cake with Strawberry Ripple Cream' from the Half Baked Harvest blog. Truly incredible.
4. Yotam Ottolenghi's cauliflower cake. Only kidding. Sounds gross.
3. 'Six-Layer Chocolate Cake with Toasted Marshmallow Filling and Malted Chocolate Frosting' from the Brown Eyed Baker, who's a Pittsburgh-based baking blogger.
2. Autumnal birthday cake by Nigella Lawson. Maple and pecan and totally delicious; this could have been number one.
1. That chocolate and salted caramel Swiss roll that someone made on *The Great British Bake Off* one time. That is so good.

Anyway, email us and we'll send you the recipe we were just talking about. It's better than all these.

Likelihood of this wish delivering happiness should it manifest: If cake did indeed make everything better that would be wonderful. Back in the real world, baking and the smell of a cake in the oven will invariably lift a mood.

49

'I WISH I FOUND IT EASIER TO MAKE SMALL TALK'

Lots of people hate making small talk – they are either slightly shy and unsure as to what to say, or consider small talk trivial and inconsequential and lacking the weight and depth of 'proper' conversation.

In reality, small talk actually serves an important purpose – it builds trust and creates the foundations for more authentic conversations and therefore deeper relationships later on.

The principal issue is people worry they will be boring or awkward, or they'll quickly run out of things to say. Such thoughts can often be self-fulfilling: if you approach a conversation with the belief it will be dull and bumbling, it probably will.

The best way to reduce awkwardness and anxiety in social situations is to put aside your own discomfort and focus all your efforts on putting whoever you're talking to at ease. That's all you need to do – forget about yourself and make your interactions all about listening, engaging and encouraging the person to whom you're talking. It will have the almost instantaneous effect of ensuring you feel much more comfortable; so seek out people who you think might be experiencing the same kind of emotions you are, and make them feel relaxed. In so doing you will cure yourself.

If this is counter-intuitive, remember the sage words of Aristotle: 'Men acquire a particular quality by constantly acting a particular way. We become just by performing just actions, temperate by performing temperate actions, brave by performing brave actions.' In other words, sometimes you have to fake it to make it.

If all else fails, remember there are huge upsides to being shy; modesty is a really attractive characteristic, your quiet impact will have a calming effect on others, and you're likely to be trustworthy, resilient and self-reliant. Those are all amazing things.

Some of literature's greatest heroes are also its most reticent – Jay Gatsby, Holden Caulfield, Jane Eyre, Frank Cauldhame, Eeyore – so email us and we'll send you a book featuring one of them.

Likelihood of this wish delivering happiness should it manifest: OK. The art of making conversation is a great one to master; the fear of standing alone in the corner at a party is likely to lead to us not going to the party in the first place.

50

'I WISH MONEY DIDN'T RULE
THE WORLD'

There are lots of wishes like this – things which sound great as idealistic 'Hey, imagine if . . .?' style sentiments, but actually make very little practical sense, sadly. Like the kind of things a group of students very new to smoking weed would half-heartedly try to discuss at 2.30 a.m., before going back to watching *Withnail and I*.

For some, a world without money sounds like a blissful Utopia, for others a naive vision a little too close to communism. What is pretty undeniable, however, is that we are all collectively conditioned by advertising, consumerist values and the relentless need to aspire; addressing our spiritual woes with material solutions whose ability to make us genuinely happy is limited at best.

So a focus on the things in life more important than money is probably no bad thing. Here's ten. Dogs. Love. Friends. Art. Cake. Time. Sex. Beaches. Family. Mountains.

But let's not be trite or naive; on a macro level, we need economic growth to create jobs, prosperity and social stability, and to alleviate poverty.

In that sense money, or growth, does rule the world, and – while there are significant environmental implications, which should not for a second be overlooked – the world becomes a more comfortable place for more people – especially in developing countries – as a result.

On an individual level, however, it is a much-repeated cliché that money doesn't equate to happiness, and earning more doesn't necessarily make you happy. That is totally true, and research has shown there is a law of steeply diminishing returns after a salary of £55,000.

There's no point hating on money, though; lots of good is done with it constantly – last year Americans gave more than a billion dollars a day to charity, and a surprising number of the world's super-rich are intending to give away the bulk of their fortunes to altruistic causes during their lifetimes.

Still worried about money's evil influence? Then get in touch and we'll send you a comprehensive guide to living off-grid.

Likelihood of this wish delivering happiness should it manifest: It's irrelevant as it's never going to happen. Sorry, hippies.

51

'I WISH I COULD GET OUT OF BED
WITH A SPRING IN MY STEP'

There's nothing more annoying than someone who bounces out of bed and starts shrieking about how happy they are to be alive and 'today is a gift, that's why it's called the present' or whatever.

At the same time, there's nothing more boring than someone muttering 'I'm not really a morning person' and slouching around disconsolately for hours in their pyjamas, whining about how they can't function without coffee.

If you can find a happy medium and have a productive start to the day, then you are way more likely to get things done and feel good about yourself.

Here's how:

★ Get a good night's sleep the night before. Sounds platitudinous and obvious. Because it is. Sorry. See Wish 60.

★ Turn the lights on as soon as you're up, then do something. Anything. There's a cool app called 'Alarmy' that forces you to complete a particular task before it shuts up. Maybe download that bad boy.

★ Set things up so your clothes are ready the night before and prepare your breakfast before you go to sleep. Minimise the decisions you need to make before your brain has had its chance to wake up properly.

★ Always make your bed. Sounds insignificant, but completing this seemingly trivial task unconsciously sets you up for a day of little achievements.

★ Drink a large glass of cold water straight away. Water fills you up, takes the edge off your appetite, which in turn makes it easier to eat something sensible for breakfast. Oats are good – they are super-versatile, slow-burn energy and are high in protein and will set you up perfectly for the day ahead. Email us and we'll send you some. We're kind like that.

Likelihood of this wish delivering happiness should it manifest: Pretty good. Having an efficient morning routine sets you up for a day where things are going to happen. Now get out there and boss it.

52

'I WISH I HAD MORE FRIENDS'

In life, you could maybe argue Friendship trumps Love.

It's often more enduring – many of us still have childhood friends yet the average romantic relationship lasts only two years and nine months.

It's less intense – it's unusual to get into a major argument with a friend; it happens, but it's not a frequent occurrence for most of us. Lots of romantic relationships are a seething hotbed of anger, resentment and mutual antipathy. Friendships aren't like that.

And Friendship is more varied – you can be friends with lots of people at once; the more the merrier, really. That's not really on in romantic relationships. Unless you're Hugh Hefner or some kind of crazed cult leader.

Despite this, it's Love that gets all the iconography; the hearts, the roses, the cupids, Valentine's Day. Poor Friendship just has those lame bracelets that fall off after about a week.

Anyway, if you're worried your friends don't love you, you're probably wrong, they just think you can be kind of needy sometimes. On the off chance you're actually correct though, here's what to do.

Be aware of the image you project; if you feel unlovable you are probably unconsciously projecting that vibe more overtly than you may realise, which creates a self-fulfilling prophesy. So maybe start work on any lurking issues related to self-esteem.

Look like you're having fun. People are drawn to people who are having a laugh; an effervescent and charismatic personality exerts a magnetic force on others. That doesn't mean you have to start randomly shrieking at things that aren't that funny, or endlessly pretending to make calls on your mobile, just ratchet the positivity up a notch or two.

Don't build walls. Metaphorical ones at least. Actual walls are fine, unless you're Donald Trump, obviously. Lots of people anticipate others may not find them desirable and therefore close themselves off as an entirely understandable defence mechanism. Be open to people and experiences. You'll get hurt once or twice, but ultimately the rewards of putting yourself out there are manifest.

If you'd like a new friend, email us a few details about yourself and we'll hook you up with someone who's in the same position.

Likelihood of this wish delivering happiness should it manifest: Huge. There is an epidemic of loneliness around the world, don't be a part of it.

'I WISH I COULD FIND A WAY TO
LIVE A SIMPLER LIFE'

OK, oh busy and conflicted one, here's what we suggest: make a list of the things that occupy your time, and study it carefully. What could you maybe sacrifice without too devastating a consequence? What are the four or five things that make you happier? Then assess that very focused list against your current situation. This means you need to undertake two kinds of analysis:

1. Your current use of time – what are you actually doing with your time? To what extent might this be altered? Is there a more efficient use of it? What can be delegated, or are there some things you can just stop doing completely? Critically, is the way you spend your time in line with your priorities as you have articulated them? If not, then start planning changes.

2. Your current set of commitments – this will likely include work, studying, family life, keeping up with friends, hobbies, civic or charity work and chores. As tricky as it may be, ask yourself which of these commitments comes with the greatest return. Which makes you happiest, but which just feel like obligations from which you haven't been able to extricate yourself?

By answering these two questions really rigorously, you can gain a clear perspective on what may be worth potentially deprioritising or eliminating altogether. To achieve this, you need to learn to say 'No' to people and demands on your time to which you might previously have agreed.

So that's what we recommend – understand what really matters, then look at your current commitments and time. Work out where the discrepancy lies and focus on eliminating it – this won't be straightforward, but will be really so worth it.

If you like, email us and we'll send you a clever technique to help create your daily to-do list and bring clarity to the age-old question of what's worth your time and what's not.

Likelihood of this wish delivering happiness should it manifest: High. The most important things in life aren't things. We saw that on Pinterest one time so it must be true.

54

'I WISH I WAS MORE PATIENT WITH
MY CHILDREN'

Even the most Zen of parents loses it with their children sometimes.

It's not a great habit – an outburst of temper leaves the child confused and isolated and the parent feeling guilty and inadequate.

That said, it's important to acknowledge that children can be – let's face it – incredibly annoying. Their endless banging on about Minecraft, persistent failure to flush the loo and repetitive enquiries as to where babies come from are enough to drive any patient adult over the edge, especially if the children concerned are not your own (the unspoken adage that, with one or two exceptions, every adult thinks most children aside from theirs are borderline sociopathic is probably true).

The best technique to maintain patience with children is to let them know you're losing it; in other words, saying really firmly 'I feel like I might get really, really cross if you don't stop licking the puppy', or whatever.

Firstly, acknowledging the impending nervous breakdown helps to keep it at bay, as just saying the words aloud is kind of therapeutic.

Secondly, even the most witless of children will usually swiftly acknowledge something about their behaviour needs to change.

The alternative – bottling up frustrated emotions until they explode – is never pretty. Yelling at a child is not only mean and increasingly socially unacceptable, it's also really ineffective as a technique for teaching them about appropriate parameters. Children are, from a young age, sufficiently astute to realise that in losing their temper the adult has stepped outside of their own level of acceptable behaviour while attempting to instil boundaries around the child's.

Having said that, if you do find yourself in the midst of some kind of crazed fit as a consequence of yet again getting hit in the eye by a plastic Minion toy, then don't be too hard on yourself. A release of temper can help recalibrate things and the day usually picks up once the air has been cleared.

If you'd like some help keeping your head when all about you are losing theirs and blaming it on you, then email us and we'll send you some dark chocolate, which has been proven to lower blood pressure.

Likelihood of this wish delivering happiness should it manifest: Pretty good. Everyone should learn to be the master or mistress of their impulses, irrespective of whether or not they are parents.

55

'I WISH I DIDN'T RECEIVE
SO MUCH JUNK MAIL'

Nothing good comes in the post anymore, unless it's from Amazon.

Sad though it may be, that statement is broadly true. Even birthday cards are dying out – Hallmark has cut its payroll from 22,000 to less than half that in five years – and it's said that within a decade the traditional Christmas card could all but disappear.

E-cards, a Facebook message or a hastily composed text are how we mark birthdays and Christmas now. The childhood cheque from Grandma is now likely to be a money transfer and her parcel an e-voucher.

With the postman's bag therefore increasingly devoid of anything exciting, we are left with utility bills, bank statements and unwanted missives, frequently addressed to 'The Homeowner' or 'The Occupier'.

Every year, Royal Mail delivers over 3.5 billion items of unaddressed post, the vast majority of which goes instantly in the bin. This means on average we now receive at least ten times more unsolicited mail than we do personal letters.

The estimated cost of junk-mail disposal to the taxpayer is thought to be well in excess of £50 million and the environmental waste is obviously enormous. At least 100 million trees are destroyed each year to produce junk mail.

In the UK, you can opt out of unsolicited mailings via the Mailing Preference Service but it is far from a comprehensive solution and will not stop mail addressed to 'The Occupier' or, obviously, discourage local businesses that put leaflets and menus through the letterbox by hand.

If you're sick of junk mail, email us and we'll send you a sticker for your letterbox. Lovingly designed, it reads: 'No junk mail. Like literally none. I don't need a pizza, a taxi or to sell my house. If I do, you'll be the first to know'.

We're not saying it will provide a magical remedy, but it may improve things.

Likelihood of this wish delivering happiness should it manifest: The absence of junk mail isn't going to change your life, let's be honest, but little domestic victories can collectively add up to a day less likely to be blighted by irritation and stress.

56

'I WISH PEOPLE WEREN'T SO
BORING ABOUT "EATING CLEAN"'

There's a strong argument to suggest we are more boring about food than at any other time in history.

Talking about your new diet is bad manners and boring. Paleo is boring; 5:2 is boring. Is there one called South Beach? Then that's boring too. Talking about how evil sugar is, and how those brownies you've made using agave syrup are just as good – they're really not, btw – is also boring.

Obsessing over your weight is boring. Not eating carbs is boring. Juicing is boring. Fasting is boring. Spurious detoxes with zero scientific rationale are boring. Insisting everything has to be organic is boring. Talking about food miles is boring. Owning a NutriBullet makes you boring. Weighing yourself every day is boring. Foraging is boring. Obsessing over things being locally sourced is boring. Talking about the importance of seasonal ingredients is boring. Talking about how much you would like to go to Noma one day is boring.

Also very boring is the requirement to share on social media everything you eat. This is especially boring if the food in question is of the kale/quinoa/goji berries/poached eggs/avocado on toast variety. Typically, these unimaginably dull postings are accompanied by an increasingly hysterical series of meaningless hashtags: #NomNomNom, #eatclean, #brunch, #health, #vegan, #nutrition, #life, #love, #happyplace, #metime, #beyourself, #IAmMe, #BeYou, etc.

The bottom line is everyone knows a funny, hedonistic, relaxed, slightly drunk person is infinitely preferable to an uptight priggish one who asks for some hot water with a 'teeny bit of lemon and some fresh ginger if you have it'. That's just a fact and Woody Allen was right when he said: 'You can live to be a hundred if you give up all the things that make you want to live to be a hundred.'

If you're in danger of being bored to death by a lame 'foodie', then email us and we'll send you some fudge. Mmm, fudge.

Likelihood of this wish delivering happiness should it manifest: Middling. Life's too short to eat 'clean', and many of the principles of the clean movement are based on flaky pseudoscience.

57

'I WISH HIGH HEELS WERE MORE COMFORTABLE'

High heels are a source of confidence, happiness and acute discomfort.

It's a fact that heels are never going to be as comfy as wearing flats, but there are occasions – the Academy Awards, your nephew's christening, Kimye's wedding – where your battered Converse simply won't cut it.

It's a frequent complaint and you have our every sympathy.

Here's how to reduce the agony in five-and-a-half steps.

1. Much of the discomfort arises from trying to stay balanced so the pointier the heel itself, the greater your potential instability. Think about swapping heels for wedges, although . . .
2. Wood and hard plastic are typically too rigid to move with your feet and don't adjust as well to uneven ground, which can make a bad situation worse at an evening event, so choose a heel with a bit more 'give' in the sole; like leather or rubber.
3. Check the position of the heel carefully – it should be directly underneath your own heel; if it's further back it won't really support your weight sufficiently and you will be thrown off balance.
4. Don't wear heels more than two days in a row – your feet need time on the ground to recover.
5. When walking in heels, keep your head up and your spine straight, like a puppet on a string (which in many ways is what you are, as a slave to the conventional, male-dominated definition of what constitutes 'beauty' – just kidding).
5½. Buy a half size too big.

Anyway, email us and we will send you a pair of invisible gel pads, which you can stick inside your favourite shoes. They help to cushion and protect sensitive areas where your shoe may rub and are really effective.

Likelihood of this wish delivering happiness should it manifest: Life-changing.
The fall of the Berlin Wall, collapse of the Soviet Union and the exit of the UK from the European Union all pale into insignificance by comparison.

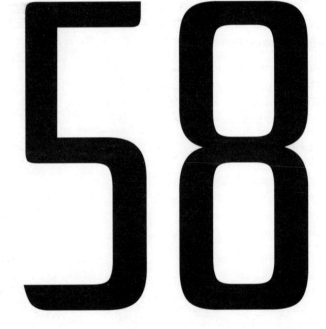

58

'I WISH I COULD DO MORE TO HELP MY MOTHER'S DEMENTIA'

Dementia is not an individual illness but a collection of symptoms caused by the brain disorders that frequently accompany old age. Its typical cause is Alzheimer's disease or a stroke. Seeing a relative suffering with dementia is awful; there is no cure and the symptoms tend to get progressively worse.

The result is that family and friends are robbed of the person they once knew. The vivacious father or contented grandmother is taken away and replaced by an unrecognisable 'other' person, whose mood may alter very suddenly, whose memory is vanishing and whose perception of the world has become tragically reduced.

In more advanced cases, sufferers become scared or aggressive for reasons that aren't easy to understand.

For a period, events from the distant past become easier to recollect than things that happened much more recently; memories fade in reverse order to when they were experienced. Eventually even these faint fragments of the past disappear altogether.

Anxiety abounds; trust disappears even between close family members or life-long friends. Taking in fresh information becomes increasingly impossible; those with dementia will be convinced they are hearing something for the first time that in reality they have been told on many occasions. The ability to read and write also disappears, compounding the feelings of loneliness and isolation.

All of these manifestations are bewildering for the sufferer and agonising and traumatic for their loved ones. Some carers have found music from the past of the patient can have a settling and therapeutic effect. Others have found sitting with the dementia patient and looking through photographs from the distant past together can also really help to create positive and clear reminisces.

If you're caring for someone with dementia, then email us a few photographs you think might resonate with the person you look after. We will print them out for you and return them by post, in the hope that looking over them together might help make this difficult condition momentarily more bearable.

Likelihood of this wish delivering happiness should it manifest: Strong. It's awful losing someone and managing dementia can be more emotionally draining than coping with bereavement.

59

'I WISH I COULD DANCE WITHOUT LOOKING DUMB'

I am the world's worst dancer. Tragic and beyond embarrassing. So much so that once, at a wedding, two strangers involuntarily yelled at me to stop and forcibly removed me from the dance floor. I pretty much decided to retire after that.

Like all creative endeavours, the thing that stifles progress is self-consciousness, our inability to relax, our feeling that we look like we might be having some kind of fit (my girlfriend's words, not mine).

We spoke to our resident DJ, the improbably named Kaiser Saucy, about how to let go. He mused for a bit then said something like:

'Don't tell me you can't dance. You can place a pencil between your thumb and forefinger and wield it with such absolute precision that you can convey language to complete strangers without even speaking. You have mastered the ability to walk and jog and run and jump with such skill and ease that you don't even stop to think about how you're achieving these gargantuan feats of physical engineering and poise. You are elegant. Music is merely the soundtrack to your perfection. Celebrate yourself. Close your eyes and feel the fundamental brilliance of your ability simply to move through the space around you. There are no right or wrong answers. There is only your imagination and your interpretation of the sound as it envelopes you. You are as agile as any panther. The only thing that's holding you back . . . is you.'

They talk like that, DJs. Especially the ones who've taken too much ketamine. That's a joke by the way. Kaiser Saucy is totally #straightedge.

Anyway, if you'd like to dance without looking dumb, you should check out Morning Gloryville, which has events all over the world. It's like a rave but it happens before work from 6.30 a.m. to 10.30 a.m; usually on a Wednesday. It's completely amazing and if you haven't been then you really should: liberated, joyous and totally anarchic, this is an essential London experience. If you don't believe us, then check out their press online.

Email us and we'll put you on the guest list for their next event.

Likelihood of this wish delivering happiness should it manifest: Short term but high. Dancing reduces stress levels and helps you to relax, stay in shape and let go.

'I WISH I COULD GET A
GOOD NIGHT'S SLEEP'

Insomnia prevents people from concentrating properly at work, impacts memory recall and increases the risk of depression and high blood pressure.

If you, like the dude from Faithless that time, can't get no sleep, then here's what you need to know, expressed in a slightly controlling and hectoring fashion:

* Once you're past adolescence, you only need seven hours sleep. Anything else is unnecessary and your brain has wrongly become accustomed to it. You are possibly entering a second cycle of sleep if you sleep too long – this is why you may wake up exhausted. So, decide when you're going to go to bed and when you're going to get up, and stick to those times. This makes weekends longer, but more productive and enjoyable.

* Cut out caffeine after 2 p.m. This includes tea, coffee, soft drinks and chocolate. Don't go to bed too full and resist the temptation to wander downstairs and start eating cold lasagne from the fridge just because you know it's there.

* The bedroom is for sex and sleep. That's it. So in the hour before bed you should avoid reading, listening to music, watching television or dicking around on your phone.

* Before you go upstairs, quickly jot down your to-do list for tomorrow in a little journal. When you've done that, close the book with an emphatic thud. The idea here is two-fold – you've planned your day ahead, so no longer have that nagging feeling you've forgotten something, and the slamming shut of the book unconsciously makes the mind less likely to disturb you while you're trying to get to sleep.

* Do three things the same every night to 'condition' your brain that sleep is coming. Make these really easy to do. They could be, say, turn the downstairs lights out; brush your teeth; pee. Whatever they are, you need to be able to always do them.

* If it takes longer than twenty minutes to sleep or if you wake up and can't get back to sleep, get up and potter around.

If you follow these steps assiduously, things will definitely get better. Email us and we'll send you the little book in which to write down the three things.

Likelihood of this wish delivering happiness should it manifest: Strong. Being robbed of sleep is a nightmare, or would be if you weren't wide awake at 3.14 a.m. and therefore incapable of dreaming.

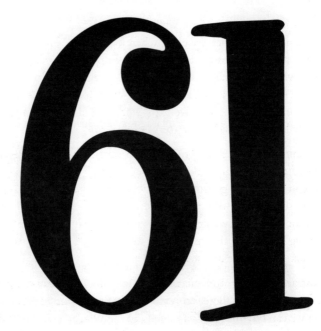

61

'I WISH I COULD BE HAPPY'

'Happiness is the whole aim and end of human existence,' Aristotle said in the fourth century BC, and since then people have been contemplating the secret of happiness and how it might be attained.

We take an empirical approach.

Researchers (specifically genius psychologist Sonja Lyubomirsky) have found approximately half of our mental well-being is down to our genes. If you're the child of two depressives, then finding day-to-day happiness is more likely to be difficult than if you're not. It's difficult to do much about that.

Only around 10 per cent of our well-being is down to our daily circumstances; how much we earn, where we live, the kind of car we drive. We tend to overestimate the positive impact of these things, which is why transformative experiences, like winning the lottery, for example, end up only having a reasonably short-term impact on our state of mind. Likewise, negative experiences – a messed-up interview, say – only have a relatively short-term impact too.

The remaining 40 per cent of our happiness is influenced by the kinds of daily activities we can all do. This is potentially interesting as it means you can maybe go from a six out of ten to a ten out of ten just by changing some simple things. The happiest people are those who have a broad social circle, are comfortable expressing gratitude, are part of something larger than themselves, lean towards an optimistic view of the future, take plenty of exercise and have a sense of meaningful purpose.

So those are the things to focus on, people. You can't alter your genetic make up (yet). Nor is there any point stressing out 'working jobs we hate so we can buy shit we don't need', in the words of Tyler Durden, as evidently that only impacts 10 per cent of our happiness. So you need to focus on the metaphysical: that's clearly where the action is.

Still struggling? Get in touch and we'll send you something that will guarantee happiness. At least momentarily.

Likelihood of this wish delivering happiness should it manifest: Reasonably high given its nature, dummy. Jesus.

62

'I WISH I COULD GET MY NOVEL PUBLISHED'

The image of the publishing industry is that it's a genteel and agreeable place, somewhat dusty and a little old-fashioned, inhabited by erudite and bespectacled types who make tea the old-fashioned way and swap *bon mots* over civilised lunches in long-established restaurants.

The reality is starkly different; publishing is as ruthless and cut-throat as any other business and completely attuned to the needs of the marketplace. Because the majority of published books fail, the industry needs big hits to offset the inevitable sequence of losers it produces.

For authors, therefore, as obvious as it sounds, the most important thing is to be working on a book people will actually want to read – writing something with commercial appeal and a clear sense of who the potential reader will be. That doesn't mean producing a manuscript that is for the lowest common denominator or derivative – more having a sense of where the market is, and how it is that you can stand out within it.

Once you've done that, the next stage is usually to find an agent, whose job it is to sell the book to editors at publishing houses. This takes time and needs proper research, but is a completely necessary step – the majority of larger publishers do not accept unsolicited work.

Having fine-tuned a list of agents you think would be a good fit, then hone your submission to them. Check their website, but this should usually comprise a two-page synopsis, the first 10,000 words of the novel itself and an overview of the project highlighting who you are, why you have written the book and why it will appeal to the audience for whom it is designed.

Most likely you will be turned down on multiple occasions by agents, and thereafter by numerous publishers to whom the agent has submitted your manuscript. Worry not. The same thing happened to John le Carré, J. K. Rowling and Stephen King. Even the book you hold in your hand, gentle reader, that too was rejected by a publishing house one time. We know, it seems crazy.

If you're determined to make it as an author, then email us and we'll help you get to the next stage, and, if you're ready, introduce you to an agent who can really make things happen.

Likelihood of this wish delivering happiness should it manifest: Possibly amazing, but, while it's not impossible, it can be pretty hard to get a book published, especially literary fiction. We would be genuinely delighted, however, to be proven wrong in your case.

63

'I WISH SOMEONE WOULD SEND
ME A HANDWRITTEN LETTER'

This wish feels like it was made by someone who is wistfully looking back to a more romantic era, when lovers slipped clandestine notes to one another, declaring their dreamy feelings on scented pages of amorous prose.

The age of digital communication has elevated letter-writing to an art form; their scarcity has ensured handwritten missives are now regarded as a rare and wonderful surprise.

There are actually quite a few very creative projects around, dedicated to the dying art of letter writing, or to re-inventing it.

Here are some of them:

* The 'Letter Writers Alliance' is a member-based organisation started in summer 2007 by Kathy Zadrozny and Donovan Beeson. It strives to give people the tools to maintain the art of letter writing.
* 'Snail Mail My Email' is cool: a worldwide community art project where volunteers handwrite strangers' emails and send physical letters to the intended recipients, free of charge.
* 'The Hand Written Letter Project' is over now but was great at the time – it extended an invitation to designers and creative thinkers alike to write and make known their thoughts in handwritten form and on their stationery. The results are really intriguing and can still be seen online.
* 'The World Needs More Love Letters' is a global organisation that lets anyone nominate someone to be the recipient of a bundle of love letters. Strangers all over the world have been surprised with beautiful and affectionate missives as a result.
* Best of all is probably Mr Bingo, who sends abusive insults via the post to those masochistic/intrigued enough to ask. Be warned, this is very rude but the invective is truly hilarious.

If you'd like a handwritten letter, then just email us your address and we'll send you one. The contents will remain a mystery until opening. You don't need to write back. This isn't some kind of pen-pal scenario, people.

Likelihood of this wish delivering happiness should it manifest: Short term, but receiving a handwritten letter is the kind of thing that makes someone's day, maybe their week. Given that a letter can be easily completed in ten minutes or less, it's definitely worth doing and seeing what comes back from the recipient.

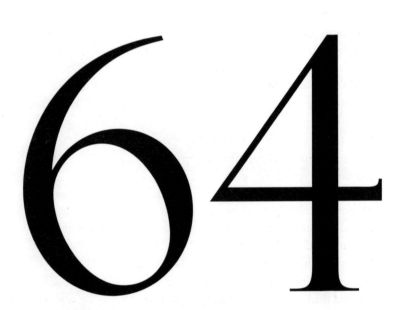

64

'I WISH THE WORLD WASN'T SO CHAOTIC AND TERRIFYING'

Right now, you could be forgiven for thinking that we stand on the edge of some kind of existential abyss, with the media consistently full of stories of terrorism, uncertainty, climate change and forthcoming economic apocalypse.

The reality is that we're in pretty good shape:

* There are half as many poor people in the world as there were in 1990 and global hunger has fallen by almost 40 per cent since 2000. Health inequality is also falling and child mortality is in rapid decline.

* Democracy is spreading – at the beginning of the twentieth century only 10 per cent of the world population lived in democratic countries – now it is more than 50 per cent.

* Economic growth is lifting poorer countries out of the poverty trap – since 1960, China's real income per person has gone up eightfold, India's has quadrupled and Brazil's has almost quintupled. Seven of the world's top-ten fastest-growing economies are now in Africa.

* The world is actually more peaceful – over history some 500 of every 100,000 people would wind up killed by another human, whether in war or otherwise. Now that number is around 6 per 100,000.

* We are also more tolerant than we have ever been; between 1995 and 2011 there was a 20 per cent decline in 'observable gender inequalities', according to the United Nations, while International Monetary Fund figures show a consistent decline in global income inequality between the sexes. Ten years ago, gay marriage didn't exist in the United States; now it's legal in the entire country after a Supreme Court ruling striking down state marriage bans.

* Without doubt young people now are more inclusive and broad-minded than previous generations; less violent, bigoted and prejudiced.

* A new generation is also spear-heading incredible innovation – developing technology to inhabit other planets, creating astonishing new transport systems, building dumbfounding artificial intelligence systems and working out how to make the internet available to the world's poorest and most remote countries.

So it's not really all bad, but if you're despairing as to the state of the world, then email us and we'll send you some chocolates to cheer you up.

Likelihood of this wish delivering happiness should it manifest: Pretty good. Don't live in fear – we're actually in better shape than ever.

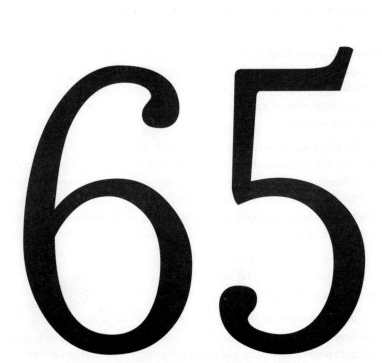

65

'I WISH WOMEN WEREN'T SO CATTY TO OTHER WOMEN'

Former US Secretary of State Madeleine Albright once remarked, 'There is a special place in hell for women who don't help other women.'

If that is the case, then that place in hell may well be pretty crowded as well as special. Despite the ongoing progress towards gender equality, there are plenty of women who believe that their worst enemies are not lumbering male chauvinists, but other women. Is it the case that the more parity between the genders is achieved, the less solidarity there is between women? And if we're headed for perpetual *Mean Girls* territory, why?

Maybe it's something to do with the fact that women have had to compete in a male-dominated environment for so long that they have – consciously or otherwise – adopted the default vernacular of that environment; one which is inherently combative and non-supportive, especially at work.

Maybe the differences between the genders aren't that acute after all and we're all just products of the stimuli to which we are exposed. Perhaps we've overdone the stereotypes about what constitutes the male/female psyche and women are as scrappy and fierce as their male counterparts. Plenty of studies have found human brains do not fit neatly into 'male' and 'female' categories.

Maybe women just take both sexes at face value and judge them on their perceived merits. The fact that women share a gender doesn't automatically mean they will be cosy kindred spirits.

Ultimately women are probably no meaner to other women than men are to other men or to women; it's just men – slightly condescendingly – expect women to be soft and empathetic, so get disproportionately freaked out on the occasions when that doesn't happen. The big babies.

If you're being bullied or intimidated by someone – of either gender – then let us know and we'll send them an envelope packed full of glitter, packed in such a way it will fall out all over their desk and floor to cause maximum inconvenience. That'll learn 'em.

Likelihood of this wish delivering happiness should it manifest: Well, no one likes cattiness, so it's absence has to be a good thing.

'I WISH I COULD TAKE
A DECENT PHOTOGRAPH'

This is the kind of thing everyone can get slightly better at, just by trying to remember a few things.

The crucial thing you need to know about is 'The Rule of Thirds'. Your phone probably has a grid feature which divides the shot into nine squares – try to put the subject of interest in your photo along the lines or where the lines cross, and your photos will naturally feel more balanced to the viewer. With portraits, place the right or left eye at the centre of the composition; this gives the impression the subject's eyes are following you.

Don't be afraid to get closer than you might initially want in order to achieve this, especially when taking photos of people, and think a little about the contrast between the object of the photo and the background. Get rid of things that are extraneous or distracting so the object of your shot has a very clear focus.

Light is everything and natural light is always best. The legendary war photographer Don McCullin once said: 'Photography isn't looking, it's feeling.' Learn to recognise great opportunities to take a photo in interesting light – often at the start and end of the day. Never shoot with the sun directly behind you. It creates boring, flat light on the subject.

Finally, never ask people to say 'cheese', like some kind of lame uncle at a naff wedding, c. 1979. It's a horrible cliché, never yields a natural grin from your subject and instantly reveals your amateur status. A well-timed joke will elicit way more authentic smiles, which in turn will exponentially improve the quality of your photograph.

If you're really serious about going to the next level as a photographer, or are thinking about it as a career choice, then email us and we'll set you up with a professional photographer for a cup of coffee and some advice.

Likelihood of this wish delivering happiness should it manifest: You'll have to wait and see but any form of creative expression has to be a good thing.

67

'I WISH MY HOUSE WASN'T SUCH A DUMP'

OK, here's how to do it, without spending an insane amount of money.

★ Invest in fresh flowers. It's a massive cliché, but they make a huge difference. That said, they are also horribly expensive, unless you buy them from Tesco, in which case they tend to be a bit depressing and only live for about half an hour. So maybe think about silk ones. Weirdly, Hobbycraft have a good selection – they are more affordable and less naff than you might imagine. Or try Freddie's Flowers, who deliver weekly bunches from just £20.

★ Buy a Råskog trolley from IKEA. They are incredible value and work in every room in the house, bringing a kind of stylish order to that which would otherwise be chaotic – books, towels, kitchen stuff, random bottles of booze. Honestly, it's the best thing IKEA has ever sold. Except the meatballs, of course, which are beyond delicious.

★ Many people find having children is the point in their lives when the chaos takes over. So find imaginative ways of dealing with all the stuff to which the little imps develop an irrational attachment. The principle of a place for everything and everything in its place has never been so important than it is during the child-rearing years.

★ We are declaring the end of the Farrow & Ball muted era of understated, muted greys and greens. Go for bright bold colours wherever possible. Find the shade you like best and ask your paint supplier to make it up for you using Leyland. This can be quite a good money-saving move and makes no material difference.

★ Create your own art by using some of the amazing libraries of photography online, which can be printed out in high resolution with no cost or rights attached. Try Unsplash to begin with and let us know if you'd like to know more about some others.

★ In a similar vein, the website freevintageposters.com has free high-resolution posters to download, many of which are total classics. The site is badly laid out and a bit annoying to use, but the content is great.

★ Plus, invest in good-quality bedding, take time to thoughtfully organise shelves, buy a scented candle once a month and remember the power of white paint.

Get in touch and we'll send you twenty suggestions for making your home look beautiful without spending a fortune.

Likelihood of this wish delivering happiness should it manifest: You might be surprised. Our surroundings and their aesthetic have a way higher influence on us than sometimes we acknowledge.

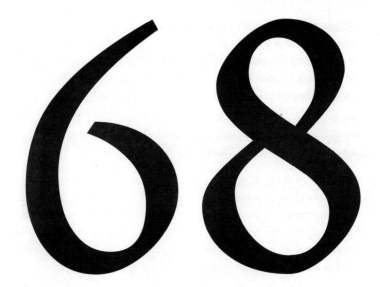

68

'I WISH I HAD LESS SOCIAL ANXIETY'

Social anxiety disorder refers to an irrational yet intense fear of social situations.

Those who suffer with this debilitating condition approach social events believing they will be embarrassed or judged or made to feel acutely self-conscious or left out.

The disorder is not just a nagging voice at the back of your mind, which everyone has to a degree, but can frequently manifest with physical symptoms like an accelerated heartbeat, the shakes, blushing or even sweating.

Stefan G. Hofmann is the director of the Social Anxiety Program at Boston University. He says:

> People are social animals, and we have a strong desire to be part of a group and to be accepted by the group. Social anxiety is a result of the fear of a possibility that we will not be accepted by our peers. It's the fear of negative evaluation by others, and that is part of a very fundamental, biological need to be liked. That's why we have social anxiety.

For those with social anxiety, seemingly innocuous events, which to others might appear to be straightforward and enjoyable – a quiz night in the pub, a lunch with colleagues – can be agonised over for days in advance.

A feeling you will be judged or disliked, or somehow found wanting, sits like a low cloud, enveloping everything. Searching for employment can be a nightmare as the idea of a job interview is too overwhelming and for many the condition is so pronounced they may find themselves increasingly avoiding social situations and becoming more and more isolated as a result. This, of course, perpetuates the anxiety.

So many people suffer with this. Anxiety disorder impacts hundreds of thousands of people in the United Kingdom, and an estimated five million in the United States.

Likelihood of this wish delivering happiness should it manifest: Huge, as many will attest. If you're one of them, please email us and we'll send you a little guide to overcoming anxiety.

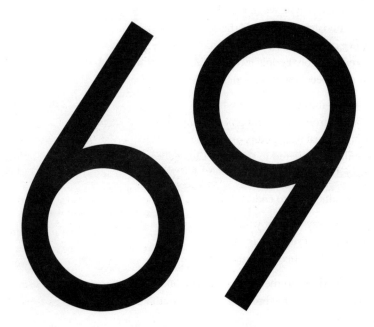

69

'I WISH I KNEW EVERYONE WHO
LIVES IN MY STREET'

This is one of those wishes that harks back to a bygone era where neighbours chatted over the garden fence and children went scrumping for apples and everyone behaved nicely because they were terrified of the Kray twins.

While those days are clearly long gone, the reality is we're more connected than ever before – it's just the communication happens via a screen. We can see each other's photographs seconds after they're taken and share each of our highly original thoughts the second they occur to us.

Yet as Facebook and Snapchat redefine how it is that we connect with each other, maybe we're realising that no amount of tweets, texts or status updates can provide the actual emotional proximity we need. Plenty of research has discovered that despite being more linked together than ever, more people feel more alone than at any other time. Britain has even been voted the loneliness capital of Europe.

Counter-intuitively, those who report feeling most alone are those you'd expect it from least: young people under thirty-five who are the most prolific social networkers of all. So there's a paradox in play; we're now umbilically tethered to those we care about most, yet we've never felt so isolated from one another.

The madness has to end, and the time to live in the real world again is now.

The best way to meet your neighbours is to organise a street party. The arrival of summer is a good excuse, as is Christmas. You'll be surprised/horrified how many turn up.

So if you'd like to meet everyone who lives in your street, email us and we'll send you some bunting, the very foundation on which street parties are built.

Likelihood of this wish delivering happiness should it manifest: Kind of depends who your neighbours are, to be honest.

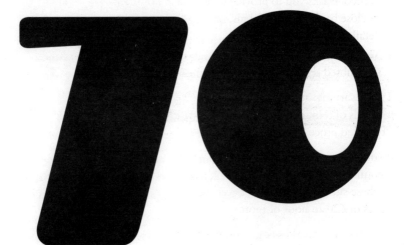

70

'I WISH I COULD WORK FROM HOME'

You totally can: remote working is a huge industry, easily worth worldwide in excess of £120 billion a year. There is a wealth of sites offering online work, but inevitably many of them are slightly dodgy and best avoided.

As a rule of thumb, here are the things that should ring alarm bells if you are looking to make money 'remote working' from home:

1. It all feels a bit too good to be true. If someone's offering untold riches for doing comparatively little, then use your abundant common sense.
2. The contracting company asks you to pay for their services upfront. If people are demanding an advance payment, don't ever make it. It undoubtedly signifies an arrangement that is not designed to benefit you.
3. Someone asks you to provide confidential information. Do not disclose bank account details, national insurance or social security details to anybody. Obvs.
4. You get the 'job' incredibly easily. Not intended as a diss on your undoubted abilities, but beware being accepted too readily.

These warnings notwithstanding, there are sites that offer legitimate methods of remote employment, pay reasonable wages and have structured processes in place to ensure nobody gets fleeced.

If you have skills and abilities in almost any area, from copywriting to accountancy, mobile-app designing to translating, there are jobs posted on these sites every minute of every day, many of which pay reasonable wages of £20 an hour or more.

1. oDesk. The world's largest online workplace.
2. Elance. Members have earned in excess of £800 million to date.
3. MyCrowd. Ten million freelancers can't be wrong.
4. Freelancer.co.uk. Almost six million available projects currently.
5. E4S. Specialises in student or gap-yah jobs.

Email us and we'll send you a guide to staying focused and productive at home, where there's no boss breathing down your neck and crapping on about how 'their door is always open' and giving you contradictory instructions and stuff.

Likelihood of this wish delivering happiness should it manifest: Strong. Get it right and you'll spend more time with family in a stress-free environment, eliminate a boring commute and see your productivity soar.

71

'I WISH I KNEW THEN WHAT I KNOW NOW'

Here – in a tiny section of a random book that until recently you had no idea even existed – are the only twenty things you need to know about life. You're welcome.

1. Unless you're literally like POTUS or something, people will generally get bored when you talk about your work.
2. What happens in the bedroom should stay in the bedroom.
3. Be miserable or motivate yourself; the choice is always yours.
4. Before you embark on a journey of revenge, dig two graves.
5. Crystals have no healing powers whatsoever.
6. People will never forget a surprise party you organise on their behalf.
7. Only a fool trips on what is behind him.
8. Don't criticise your body.
9. Life is comprised of tiny, apparently insignificant little things, not momentous, earth-shattering events.
10. Monty Python is overrated, so are Lady Gaga, weddings and the four things to which Christopher Hitchens referred.
11. This too shall pass.
12. Your sense of fluctuating self-esteem is only interesting up to a point, even to those who love you most.
13. The best song ever written is called 'Under Cover of Darkness' by New York quartet The Strokes. Or maybe 'Tiny Dancer' by Elton John. Or maybe 'Life on Mars' by David Bowie. Definitely one of those.
14. It's true that children grow up amazingly quickly.
15. Your boss is going to be a bit of dick sometimes, and you're going to have to deal with that.
16. Read *One Hundred Years of Solitude* by Gabriel José de la Concordia García Márquez.
17. Realise and accept life isn't fair.
18. Make peace with your parents.
19. People with nothing to lose will stop at nothing to win.
20. Don't sweat the small stuff. It's all small stuff.

Email us and we'll send you the words above, lovingly typeset, to hang up somewhere.

Likelihood of this wish delivering happiness should it manifest: Good. You shall know the truth and the truth shall set you free.

72

'I WISH THE WEEKEND WAS LONGER
THAN THE WORKING WEEK'

It's not the craziest idea in the world. In fact, it's a point of view that has way more traction and credibility than you might imagine.

The Ford Motor Company, pioneers in improving workers' conditions in the 1920s, was the first major manufacturing company to reduce the working week from six to five days.

More recently, when the US state of Utah was hit hard by the recession in 2008 inevitably unemployment rose, productivity declined, housing foreclosures increased and public money urgently needed to be saved. The Governor of Utah at the time, Jon Huntsman, decided that if all the state-sector workers were to work a shorter week, he could close all public buildings on the fifth day and thereby save a fortune. At only four-weeks' notice, 18,000 of the state's 25,000 workers were put onto a four-day week, and 900 public buildings closed on Fridays. State vehicles remained stationary on the fifth day, eventually saving three million motoring miles.

After a short period of adjustment there were almost no complaints. Eight out of ten employees loved this initiative and wanted it to continue. Two-thirds claimed it increased their productivity; just 3 per cent said it created childcare problems. Offices all around Utah reported a surge in staff morale. The alteration saved the state millions of dollars. Congestion was reduced and carbon emissions fell by 14 per cent.

Despite these positive examples, a four-day week is unlikely to be adopted as the approach taken by most businesses, sadly. How then to solve the issue? For most of us the problem comes from mentally dividing the week up into work and non-work – we slog through five days of mind-numbing grind to attain the reward of two days off. Repeat to fade. It's no way to lead to a life.

As trite as it may sound, the solution lies in finding something at which you're brilliant, becoming even better at it and then ingeniously finding a way to make a living from it. That way, the division between 'work' and 'play' becomes blurred; rather than work being something to endure it becomes a mission, a real reason for being, an inspiring purpose.

If you're struggling to find your true north, email us some details about yourself and we'll help you find your calling.

Likelihood of this wish delivering happiness should it manifest: Not bad, but in practical terms unlikely, unless of course you start your own venture – see Wish 1.

73

'I WISH I DIDN'T GIVE UP SO EASILY'

If you haven't read Steven Pressfield's *The War of Art*, we're not going to judge. It's pretty obscure. It contains some essential wisdom, however, and that is this: 'The more important a call or action is to our soul's evolution, the more resistance we will feel toward pursuing it.'

* George Lucas was rejected by over twenty film companies before getting a green light for *Star Wars*.
* Had J. K. Rowling quit – after writing all day in cafés, living on benefits with her daughter and being rejected by multiple publishers – we would have no Harry Potter.
* Albert Einstein didn't speak until he was four and didn't read until he was seven. He had a difficult time at school and was not given a place at his chosen Polytechnic School in Zurich.
* Walt Disney was fired from the *Kansas City Star* in 1919 because, his editor said, he 'lacked imagination and had no good ideas'. Later in his career his cherished plans for a theme park were rejected 302 times.
* During his lifetime Vincent van Gogh received virtually no acclaim for his work. He only sold one of his paintings, and that was to a friend for a very small amount of money.
* Howard Schultz had 242 banks turn down his Starbucks business plan.
* Over 200 investors said no to Google.
* Atari founder Nolan Bushnell turned down the chance to buy a third of Apple for $50,000, or about £40,000 (that stake today would be worth around $250,000,000,000 or £195,000,000,000).
* Dick Rowe of Decca Records dismissively told Brian Epstein, 'Guitar groups are on their way out', before failing to sign The Beatles.

Nobody knows anything, so whatever it is you're doing, hang in there and don't quit. If you feel like quitting, then email us with your concerns and we'll send you some personalised advice and encouragement.

Likelihood of this wish delivering happiness should it manifest: High. Tenacity is an invaluable quality to develop.

74

'I WISH I COULD MAKE MY OWN FURNITURE'

We love this wish, mainly because it brings to mind Ron Swanson, the hero of the legendary TV series *Parks and Recreation* (worth adding to the list of great shows in Wish 17).

Anyway, everyone should be able to, at the very least, make a small chair. Just as they should know how to wire a plug, grow their own vegetables, jump-start a car, deliver bad news, perform the Heimlich Manoeuvre, ask for a pay rise, shuck an oyster, hang a picture, tell a good story, pack properly for a holiday, use chopsticks, teach a child to ride a bike, land a punch, build a fire, make a good first impression, sew on a button, break down a door, back-up a hard drive, get out of the friend zone, poach an egg, split a log, detect a lie, get rid of a red-wine stain, take a compliment, let go of regret, apologise sincerely, gut and clean a fish, change a flat tyre, unhook a bra, give precise directions, paint a room, look after a baby for an afternoon, parallel park, take criticism, buy a diamond, bandage a wound, set up a wireless network, remove a splinter, negotiate a bargain, speed read, say 'I love you', bake a cake, use a fire extinguisher, treat a bee sting, bake a pie, host a barbecue, complete a tax return, get into a nightclub, make a child laugh, mix a delicious cocktail, dress appropriately for the occasion, know what the first rule of Fight Club is, neatly wrap a present and flirt without scaring the object of your affection.

These are essential life skills, people.

If you'd like to try and make a chair, then email us.

We'll send you some simple instructions and a random tool. A hammer maybe. Possibly a chisel.

Likelihood of this wish delivering happiness should it manifest: Possibly dependent on the outcome of the endeavour, but there's a high degree of satisfaction to be gleaned from making anything well.

75

'I WISH I COULD CONTROL
MY MIGRAINES'

In the UK, there are an estimated 190,000 migraine attacks every day. Those who suffer with them will know just how awful they are.

You will know if you are having a migraine (calling them 'headaches' doesn't even come close; a migraine is way more intense): you'll have a recurrent throbbing that often affects one side of the head and is frequently accompanied by nausea and disturbed vision. Typically, migraines last anything from a couple of hours to three days. They also leave a residual, draining effect, so even when they're over, they're kind of not.

Severe migraine attacks are classified by the World Health Organization as among the most disabling illnesses; comparable to dementia and even psychosis.

Migraines are believed to be caused by a mixture of environmental and genetic factors; about two-thirds of the time they run in families. There was a time when it was considered that only the very intelligent suffered with migraines but this is no longer thought to be the case, removing even that small consolation from those who live with this debilitating condition. Physical activity may intensify the pain, but symptoms can vary from person to person and from one attack to the next.

There is no known 'cure' for migraines, but certain herbs can be helpful for some sufferers, among them chamomile, which is a great remedy for stress, nerves and anxiety. It has an anti-inflammatory effect on the body, and can sometimes help with certain types of headaches.

Email us and we'll send you some chamomile teabags. Obviously this is not some miraculous remedy, and anyone who has to endure frequent severe headaches should definitely be speaking to their doctor about the best course of action. We totally realise this is a token gesture if ever there was one; those who live with migraines have all our sympathy.

Likelihood of this wish delivering happiness should it manifest: Well, if there was a definitive cure, which hopefully one day soon there will be, it would be amazing for those who endure migraines.

76

'I WISH THAT OLDER
PEOPLE WEREN'T SO
OFTEN LONELY'

Mother Teresa once said: 'The biggest disease today is not leprosy or cancer or tuberculosis, but rather the feeling of being unwanted, uncared for and deserted by everybody.'

Most developed nations have an ageing population and the UK is no exception; in fact, there are more pensioners than there are children under sixteen and almost one in five people will live to see their hundredth birthday.

According to the charity Age Concern UK, four million older people consider the TV to be their main form of companionship, a million pensioners go a month without any form of human contact and 600,000 only leave their house once a week or less.

A recent report stated, with some credibility, that loneliness has become a major health issue in this country, with people who feel isolated twice as likely to die prematurely as those who don't. Being lonely is arguably more detrimental to your health than obesity. It is also a state that creates a host of other emotions – from depression to anger. These in turn exacerbate a fear of rejection, which leads to people cutting themselves off still further and the vicious cycle intensifies.

For many people, their 'twilight' years can be an unfairly downbeat experience; faculties are stripped away, mobility decreases, activity levels decline, comforting memories fade. It is truly bleak for millions.

If you know someone who lives alone and you think they might benefit from a visit, let us know and we'll send you some chocolates to take around to them. Now you have no excuse.

While you're there, maybe talk to them about the many apps that are great for the older generation ('Senior's Phone', 'Words with Friends', 'Gogo Grandparent') and how investing in a tablet or smartphone might help them to stay in touch with distant friends or relatives.

Likelihood of this wish delivering happiness should it manifest: Amazing, especially for the person you're visiting.

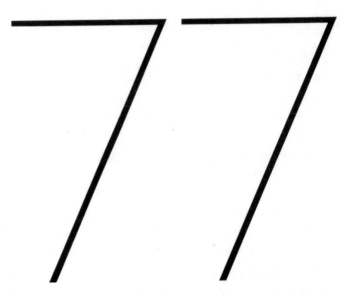

77

'I WISH THAT EVERYBODY UNDERSTOOD OBSESSIVE COMPULSIVE DISORDER'

'I'm a little bit OCD' is a phrase that is increasingly used these days, usually intended in a jokey way about being slightly uptight or controlling over something like cleaning.

The reality of obsessive compulsive disorder is very different and about as far away from amusing as any condition can be. OCD is a disorder of the brain and behaviour. It involves both obsessions and compulsions that are clearly irrational, yet to sufferers seem both alarmingly real and impossible to escape from.

These might include irrational fears of germs or illnesses, in some cases so extreme that even hugging a relative becomes impossible. Some sufferers are compelled towards ritualistic acts like compulsive hand washing or arranging objects in particular sequences. Vital signs like heartbeats may be measured obsessively. Sufferers can become haunted by repetitive thoughts about dying or those closest to them being in danger.

As sufferer Toni Neville puts it:

> It's like being controlled by a puppeteer. Every time you try and just walk away he pulls you back. Are you sure the stove is off and everything is unplugged? Back up we go. Are you sure your hands are as clean as they can get? Back ya go. Are you sure the doors are securely locked? Back down we go. How many people have touched this object? Wash your hands again.

Those tortured by OCD are in a constant battle to escape from their fears, and seek to control them through obsessive acts that typically become more extreme unless they seek professional help.

The fact that the fear is irrational does not diminish its power and the extent of its grasp over an individual is really difficult to convey. It is also a very difficult condition for those who love or live with sufferers to deal with.

As OCD expert David Adam says: 'I'm not a psychiatrist, I'm not a psychologist, but the one thing I can guarantee is it won't go away by itself. It's a medical problem, so you must seek out medical help.'

If you're worried you have obsessive compulsive disorder, email us and we will send you a journal to record unwelcome or repetitive thoughts, and the things you do to combat them. It really helps to objectify the patterns and to understand what might help to overcome them.

Likelihood of this wish delivering happiness should it manifest: High. OCD is widely misunderstood and its appropriation into the popular vernacular hasn't really assisted its understanding.

78

'I WISH I COULD LEARN TO PLAY THE GUITAR'

Lots of people dream of learning to play the guitar. There's the irreplaceable sense of musical accomplishment and feeling of satisfaction in mastering something new. Music is a fantastic outlet for creativity, self-expression and inspiration.

But we all know those are irrelevant by-products.

The real reason is that playing guitar is the easiest way into a band and being in a band is the best place in the world to be.

Seriously, no other career option offers the potential that belonging to a successful band does.

The crazed fans, the private jets and zoos, the endless trips to rehab, the sex tapes, the patient presence of a pained but long-suffering wife, the smuggling of a mountain lion into your luxury hotel suite, the tattoos that probably weren't the best idea but felt right at the time, the deep-fried banana and peanut-butter sandwiches, the brawling with record company executives, the arrest for public indecency, the ill-advised plastic surgery, the abandoning of your pet monkey at customs, the incident in the Holiday Inn that dare not speak its name, the incident where you run yourself over before placing the blame on one too many jacket potatoes, the throwing of raw offal into the audience, the siring of multiple illegitimate offspring, the descent into full-on madness, the purchase of a hovercraft before stalling it on some railway tracks, the merciless assault with a sex toy on a roadie, The Spaghetti Incident, the invasion of the stage having decided the wrong person has won an award, the astonishing comeback and the ultimate enshrining as a bona fide legend.

All this awaits you. You just need to get started.

As if the above were not incentive enough, email us with the identities of the rock stars behind each of the above incidents and we'll send you a plectrum to get you started. We accept some may have more than one perpetrator. We also accept that a plectrum is a truly terrible prize. Sorry. So sorry now.

Likelihood of this wish delivering happiness should it manifest: It varies. For some the ascent to Rock God status is literally a death sentence; others seem to cope pretty well.

79

'I WISH I COULD GET OVER MY FOMO'

FOMO (Fear Of Missing Out) refers to the feeling of anxiety 'that an exciting or interesting event may currently be happening elsewhere'. The trend is now so widespread the acronym was added to the *Oxford English Dictionary* in 2013.

It's a pathetically obvious point, but the FOMO phenomenon has been enormously accelerated by social media. When someone's new engagement sparkles tauntingly on your Instagram feed, a dumbass automated email from LinkedIn just informed you that your junior school nemesis just made CEO and some douche is furiously Snapchatting from a rooftop pool party to which you weren't invited, then you're going to start to feel a little jangly. Secretly we know that the events in question aren't quite as perfect as their lovingly filtered appearance makes them out to be, but we still feel sad.

In the most acute cases, FOMO prevents us from enjoying what's going on around us and makes us miss out on the present. We either overcommit and fail to fulfil many of those commitments, or choose to not even make arrangements or plans in the first place, fearing our choice of brunch venue/breed of puppy/new boyfriend/holiday destination/chosen career/distressed knitted sweater will be usurped by someone else's.

How then to best cope with FOMO? Hold this truth dear; needs are limited but desires are endless. Accepting the essential futility of trying to fulfil every desire we have is much wiser than indulging all of our impulses for gratification. Prioritising certain activities enables us to let go of others, so decide what your highest priorities are and focus on them. (FYI, the word 'decide' comes from the Latin '*decidere*', which means 'to cut off'.) In other words, learn to say No.

FOMO itself is a massively 2013 thing anyway; these days it's all about MOMO (Mystery Of Missing Out) – the suspicion you are not invited to events that are so cool they would never be seen on something as vanilla as Instagram, in the style of Kate Moss's birthday party at Claridge's that time.

Email us and we'll comp you membership of an app that curates genuinely cool things to do, many of which would never appear needily on social media.

Likelihood of this wish delivering happiness should it manifest: Medium. The kind of people who are desperate to get invited to particular parties are the very people that make those parties so lame in the first place.

80

'I WISH I HAD CLEARER SKIN'

Spots are meant to be things that just happen to us during adolescence, a teenage rite of passage along with throwing up after too many blue WKDs, watching PewDiePie, slamming bedroom doors and pretending you know what's going on in *Donnie Darko*.

However, it turns out – somewhat unfairly – you actually get spots all the way through life, which is bloody annoying and completely defeats the purpose of growing up.

Anyway, listen up to our five incredibly boring tips and you'll notice the benefits within five or six years. Only kidding; the results will be instantaneous. Almost.

1. The worst crime you can commit is to go to sleep with your make-up on. Well, not the worst crime, that would be murder or something, but leaving greasy slap on your face overnight clogs pores and prevents skin from breathing properly.

2. Coming up, a candidate for the most pious sentence ever written. Eat more berries: they contain lots of antioxidants and vitamin C and a low Glycaemic Index, so they won't elevate your blood sugar levels (told you). Sugar can lead to spots, so try and snack on berries instead.

3. Spots are caused by excess oil in the skin, and excess oil is often produced if your skin feels dehydrated. So drink more water. Literally the dullest advice in history is 'drink more water'. Sorry.

4. Oil from your hair gets onto your pillowcase as you're sleeping every night, so change your pillowcases every week to prevent this from happening. You should be doing this anyway, you total slattern.

5. Without wanting to sound like some kind of Howard Hughes-style germ obsessive, there are bacteria all around us. You pick them up from phones, menus, buttons, public spaces; everywhere. Avoid endlessly touching your face – in an attempt to be coquettish or whatever – and you avoid transferring them.

Finally, tea tree oil can be really good for spots and pimples, so email us and we'll send you some to help the next time your skin gets all teenage on you. You're welcome.

Likelihood of this wish delivering happiness should it manifest: Seems trivial, but spots are deeply annoying and steal self-confidence from those who are cursed with them.

81

'I WISH PEOPLE WOULD
STOP LEAVING DOGS IN
OVERHEATED CARS'

It's amazing this still happens, but every year there are still thousands of incidents of dogs dying when left unattended in vehicles.

There's a common misconception that the people who do this must be cruel or neglectful owners. On the majority of occasions this is not the case at all – they are people who love their dogs and are enjoying a day out with them. They're just regular people who make a mistake, usually an underestimation of the time it's going to take them to complete their chores, which means the dog is left alone too long.

The issue is that the speed at which a dog can develop breathing difficulties is way more rapid than people realise. In the time it takes to pick up a few things for dinner at the supermarket and get through the checkout, a dog left in a hot car could have already died or suffered brain damage, even when it is in the shade, a window is open and there is water available.

Nor does it have to be especially warm outside for a car to become dangerously hot inside – when it's 27°C outside, the temperature inside your car can heat up to 37°C within ten minutes.

Beating the heat is very difficult for dogs because they can only cool themselves by panting and by sweating through their paw pads. If the air around them is too hot – particularly if they don't have access to water – dogs are physically unable to regulate their body temperature and will very rapidly begin to struggle.

The best thing is always to take your dog with you, even if you think you'll only be a couple of minutes.

If this is an issue that worries you, email us and we'll send you a striking poster to pin up in your local community. If even one dog gets saved, it will be worth it. Yes, we know it's pious when people say that.

Likelihood of this wish delivering happiness should it manifest: Obviously high. Dogs losing their lives in this way is completely avoidable and horrible.

82

'I WISH I WAS A MORE
CAPABLE COOK'

Don't worry about that. All you need do is master one recipe that is sufficiently delicious to create the impression it's just one of many you're capable of rustling up. Here's one:

★ Go to an old-school fishmonger a few days beforehand. Ask them for some fillets of black cod. If they look at you blankly, then explain condescendingly it's also known as sablefish.

★ Next, get yourself to a decent supermarket. Buy salad leaves, something called mirin,* a little bottle of sake, some miso paste and some dark sesame oil.

★ Go home and have a cup of tea or something. Then combine 50 ml of mirin and the same volume of sake in a little saucepan. Bring it to the boil and keep it there for twenty seconds, before turning the heat down and stirring in three tablespoons of the miso paste and a tablespoon of sugar. Casually whisk for a bit and let the sugar dissolve.

★ Take it off the heat and whisk in two teaspoons of the sesame oil. Transfer to an ovenproof bowl and let the mixture cool down. Reward yourself with a vodka tonic, irrespective of the time of day. You deserve it and don't let anyone judge you.

★ Meanwhile, add the fish fillets to the mixture and turn them over a few times. Then cover the dish with clingfilm and put it in the fridge for up to a day while you try and remember the names of some friends you can tolerate having over for dinner.

★ When your guests eventually materialise, remove the fillets from the fridge, gently shake off any excess marinade and grill for two to three minutes on each side, until their surface goes brown and starts to crisp up. The fish should look kind of opaque and be pulled apart easily with a fork.

Strangely this recipe, while being fish based, actually goes best with fruity red wines like Zinfandel or Cru Beaujolais. Who knew? (As people used to say about eighteen months ago, annoyingly.)

Serve with the leaves and maybe some rice if you can be bothered, before bathing luxuriantly in a sea of compliments and passing out from excess Zinfandel.

Get in touch and we'll send you fifty easy recipes which look more sophisticated than they actually are.

Likelihood of this wish delivering happiness should it manifest: Well, everyone should be able to cook at least one thing just to qualify as a functioning adult. Scrambled eggs don't count.

* Like a rice wine or something apparently.

83

'I WISH I COULD PAY BACK MY PARENTS FOR ALL THEY'VE GIVEN ME'

What, like literally? That will be £230,000 according to analysts at the Centre for Economics and Business Research who found that was the average cost of bringing up a child from birth to aged eighteen. Although that sounds like a woeful underestimate to us, and only slightly less than we were forced to spend when we made the mistake of suggesting to our nephews we spend the afternoon at Legoland that time.

There have been some cases of parents issuing invoices to their children, usually after their offspring hit the big time financially, but it's not the standard practice. The unspoken agreement is that your parents look after you in your formative years, then you look after them during their dotage, which seems way more civilised and compassionate.

In terms of expressing appreciation for all your parents have done, it's pretty straightforward really.

They want to feel loved, appreciated and valued. Parents have earned the right to be treated with patience and understanding. Avoid being grouchy with them or snapping because your ageing father doesn't share your perspective on the EU or hasn't quite grasped the point of Snapchat yet.

Parents want to hear from their children regularly, and not just via a routine or tokenistic telephone call with some cursory summary of another standard week. They want to know what's really happening in your life, and if you share that with them there's a very real chance they will have something perceptive and helpful to add. On the occasions their advice is wide of the mark, then be diplomatic and just murmur appreciatively.

Finally, avoid telling your parents what to do – if you try to parent a parent, it's going to go badly for everyone. Just because your elderly mother may need help in one area, it doesn't make her ineffectual or hopeless in others, so don't make that assumption. It's demeaning and takes away independence.

If you'd like to show appreciation for your parents, then email us and we'll send them a beautiful, personalised print on your behalf, expressing – in a non-cheesy way – how much they mean to you. You know what they say about a picture being worth a thousand words.

Likelihood of this wish delivering happiness should it manifest: High. One day, the chance to express appreciation will be gone forever. Take it while you can.

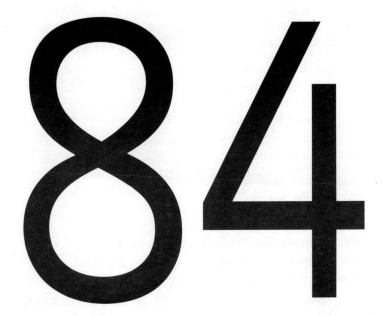

84

'I WISH PARENTS TOOK MORE TIME TO READ TO THEIR CHILDREN'

Only around half of children regularly receive a bedtime story. That seems a little sad.

We would obviously never tell anyone – parent or non-parent – what they should be doing with their time, although there is no doubt a bedtime story with a child can be a really magical experience.

The extent to which this is a lost tradition is difficult to quantify, but it's definitely an easier element to introduce to your routine if both parent and child love the story in question.

Reading aloud to a child provides a magical moment of stillness and creates a beautiful bond between adult and child. It's cosy and soothing – a routine, a mark of punctuation that is both reassuring and therapeutic for a young child.

A bedtime story also cultivates a child's imagination in a way movies can't; the pictures they see in their minds are always the most detailed and vivid. If they're really young, then stories are helpful for learning colours, counting, identifying shapes and understanding more about the world. It also encourages a love of reading, which in turn helps with writing and cognitive development more broadly.

Anyway, if you're in need of inspiration, here are the best children's books of all time. Maybe.

1. *Father Christmas* (Raymond Briggs)
2. *The Giant Alexander* (Frank Herrmann)
3. *The Adventures of Mrs Pepperpot* (Alf Prøysen)
4. *The Tiger Who Came to Tea* (Judith Kerr)
5. *The Velveteen Rabbit* (Margery Williams and William Nicholson)
6. *Stig of the Dump* (Clive King)
7. *James and the Giant Peach* (Roald Dahl)
8. *Charlotte's Web* (E. B. White)
9. *Eloise at the Plaza* (Kay Thompson)
10. *Haunted House* (Jan Pieńkowski)

Get in touch and we'll send you a children's book to read to the little person in your life.

Likelihood of this wish delivering happiness should it manifest: This sounds horribly cloying but reading with a child is a wonderfully restful experience and a ritual they love.

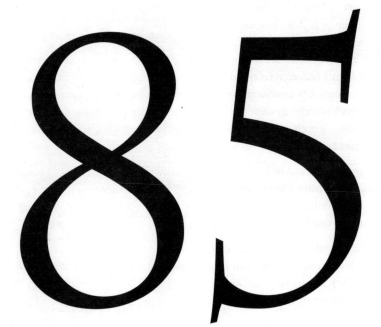

85

'I WISH I COULD BECOME A MODEL'

Modelling seems like a seductive career choice: well paid, glamorous, foreign travel, lots of people laughing at your jokes, lighting your cigarettes and endlessly telling you how pretty you are.

In reality, it's a shady, abusive business masterminded by predatory men, where eating disorders are tacitly encouraged, incredibly young girls are bullied and manipulated, and where drug and alcohol abuse is rife: an ugly industry masquerading as a beautiful one.

It's particularly depressing given most models start work between the ages of thirteen and sixteen. The majority of models receive little support and many report not even being chaperoned to jobs or go-sees. Models report that drug use in the workplace is rampant, as is sexual harassment and abuse. Typically, this goes unreported and if agents are told, typically, they are unsympathetic. Models have even reported that their agents encouraged them to sleep with their harassers to help boost their careers. On a more day-to-day basis, it's a standard expectation that models will – in clear view of what are essentially a bunch of strangers – get changed in public with nothing to protect their modesty at shows and photo shoots.

According to the Model Alliance – a New York-based advocacy group seeking to create a safer, fairer environment for models – two-thirds of models have been pressured to lose weight by their agencies and more than two-thirds of models say they suffer from anxiety or depression.

While the salaries at the high end can be amazing, less established models are frequently fleeced by the agencies – last year several leading New York model agencies were sued by former models for 'creating a secretive environment that leaves them in the dark about financial matters'.

Even the Queen of the Catwalk, Cara Delevingne, has described the industry as 'horrible'.

If you're in any doubt as to the reality then seek out the documentaries *Picture Me* or *Girl Model*, both of which are available online.

If you're still not convinced, then email us and we'll make some non-patronising suggestions for less damaging career paths.

Likelihood of this wish delivering happiness should it manifest: Almost non-existent. If you'd like to be exploited in almost every conceivable way, then modelling is the industry for you.

86

'I WISH MY PARTNER*
DIDN'T SNORE SO MUCH'

* Apologies for using that horribly annoying word.

What a douche. Only kidding, sure they're lovely.

This is a wish many people – statistically speaking mostly wives and girlfriends – will be sympathetic towards as new research reveals that 90 per cent of people live with a snoring partner.

Snoring can affect people of all ages, including children, although it's more common in middle-aged adults, especially men, twice as many of whom snore than women.

Snoring is deeply unsexy and a massive pain for the person who's sharing the bed with you. It's also the kind of thing that exacerbates any existing cracks that may be in a relationship – if you can cause the person you live with to resent you even while you're sleeping, then what chance do you have of avoiding their withering gaze while you're awake?

Without being too gross about it, snoring is caused by the vibration of soft tissue in your head and neck as you breathe in and out during sleep. This includes the nasal passages, the soft palate in the roof of your mouth and your tonsils. It's a difficult thing to cure, although it can be better managed.

Even having surgery is no guarantee of 'curing' the problem, nor do nasal strips really work, and while factors such as losing weight and quitting smoking can help alleviate snoring, they won't ensure it never happens again, so pay no heed to those who peddle miracle cures.

The only thing that consistently seems to help is radically to cut back on alcohol intake – too much booze causes excessive muscle relaxation, which makes snoring more likely. So, as tedious as it may initially seem, try an alcohol-free evening or two and see if it helps.

In the absence of a sure-fire solution, get in touch and we'll send you a pair of earplugs, which you can gleefully present to your long-suffering partner.

Likelihood of this wish delivering happiness should it manifest: Well, for the poor individual who has the misfortune to share the bed with you, high.

87

'I WISH I WAS BETTER AT JOB INTERVIEWS'

Rare is the person who relishes the prospect of a job interview.

The racing heart, the nervous palpitations, the awkward handshake; interviews are a nightmare.

There's always a terrible fear of blurting out something incredibly inappropriate in the manner of the candidate we heard about who, when asked why he had left his previous role, explained he strongly resented 'being forced to attend anger management classes'.

According to recent research, 33 per cent of interviewers know whether or not they will hire applicants within thirty seconds of meeting them, so the old adage about first impressions really counting is definitely true. Like many situations in life, preparation is everything. Know your stuff and be charming to everyone you meet, from a receptionist to a PA. Tell good stories, exude self-belief and dress the part.

If you get the chance to schedule the interview, then apparently 10.30 a.m. on Tuesday is the optimum time. That way you're avoiding Mondays where employees typically feel overworked and harassed, and also avoiding the end of the week when they're likely to be in 'wind down' mode. For the same reason, avoid the first and last calendar slots in the day. Right before lunch the interviewer may be too hungry to really focus on your genius, right afterwards they could be sluggish. So 10.30 a.m. Tuesday it is.

If you have an interview coming up, then get in touch.

If convenient, you can come in to our London offices to hone your interview technique and get some tips on completely nailing your next encounter with a prospective employer. Like the genius response (again, told to us anecdotally) from the person who, during that awful bit at the end of the 'conversation' when you're meant to ask intelligent questions enquired: 'If I get an offer, how long will it be before I have to take the drugs test?'

Amazing.

Likelihood of this wish delivering happiness should it manifest: Potentially huge. If you can master your nerves, you're more than halfway there.

88

'I WISH I COULD GET THAT NOVEL FINISHED'

One of the reasons for this wish – to be momentarily cynical – is there is a subtle but important difference between wanting to write a novel and wanting to be someone who has written a novel. Being a writer comes with significant social cachet; it's a sign of intelligence, wit and romanticism. Lots of people would like to be seen that way and a novel provides a reasonable shortcut.

It should go without saying that if that is your motivation – consciously or otherwise – then the novel will most likely fail and it may explain why the first draft is currently on the shelf, unattended and unloved.

But presupposing you're in it for legitimate reasons and have started, it's worth being honest with yourself as to why you've stopped. If it's because you've just lost enthusiasm for the project artistically, then that's a bad sign – if the writer of a novel can't really be bothered with it, then it's unlikely any hypothetical readers ever will.

It may be, however, that your passion for the project is undiminished and you're just suffering with writer's block. This is the curse of many novelists, including David Nicholls, whose novel *Us* was published in 2014 to much acclaim. Having sold five million copies of his previous work, *One Day*, Nicholls found himself so paralysed by writer's block when writing his new book, he resorted to downloading 'Write or Die', a software package which starts deleting your words if you don't write enough within a set time frame. Yikes.

This isn't a very original insight but, like lots of goals, completing a novel is a task that seems super-intimidating when seen in its entirety, so, as with anything, the key is to break it down into achievable micro steps. It's easier to commit to writing 250 words a day for a year than it is to say 'I am going to write a 100,000-word novel'. The work is accomplished one word at a time.

We get that even that kind of commitment can be tricky to maintain, so if you're serious about finishing your novel, email us and we'll send you some Post-it notes – essential for plotting structure.

Likelihood of this wish delivering happiness should it manifest: High. There's definitely a high level of satisfaction to be gleaned from the completion of any creative endeavour.

89

'I WISH I DIDN'T HAVE SO MANY REGRETS'

In life we're not meant to have regrets.

We're somehow conditioned to believe that we shouldn't look backwards, that it's more positive not to dwell on the past but instead keep moving and regret nothing.

Carpe diem, right? Or, as the kids used to say, YOLO.

But as a philosophy to live by, how achievable or worthwhile is a regret-free existence?

Is it inherently a negative thing to look back at a particular incident and feel remorseful, or apologetic or slightly ashamed? Is that not just proof of the fact that we care, that we want to avoid the same mistakes? That doesn't seem like a bad way to be.

Of course, endlessly fixating over that which has gone wrong is no way to exist either, but barrelling blithely through life, blissfully free of remorse, believing that all our decisions are great because they 'felt right at the time', can't be good.

Instead of not having regrets, or trying to pretend we don't, maybe it's better to face up to them, and to assess what might have been different or what insight our regrets provide about ourselves. We appreciate this advice is a little self-helpy, sorry.

They don't have to be crippling, but regrets can actually be really useful if addressed directly. One way to do this is to write out a list – it helps to acknowledge them fulsomely, deal with their consequences, forgive yourself and let go. Email us and we'll send you a beautiful notebook in which to do just that.

The 'No regrets' thing is up there (or down there) with the worst of the clichéd, fridge-magnet style philosophies that attempt glibly to summarise what life is in a cutesy sentence. Here are the five most facile:

1. 'Life is what happens to you while you're busy making other plans'.
2. 'Everything happens for a reason'.
3. 'Live, laugh, love'.
4. 'If life gives you lemons, make lemonade'.
5. 'Life is not about waiting for the storm to pass. It's about learning to dance in the rain'.

Likelihood of this wish delivering happiness should it manifest: Learning to live with or even benefit from regret has to be a good thing.

90

'I WISH MY CHILDREN LISTENED TO EVEN HALF OF WHAT I SAID'

Children lack peripheral awareness. If they're engaged in a game, watching TV or immersed in some alternative universe via their iPad, they probably can't hear you that well. Relax.

The key is not to shout some vague instruction up the stairs and then expect a perfect and prompt response. You need instead to get down on their level, look them in the eye, speak super-clearly, and use their name in a calm and stable fashion. 'Araminta,' you must say, 'please put down the knife, or there will be no screen time for up to three minutes.'

The rules of communication between adult and child are just the same, really, as they are between adults. Don't interrupt. Get the volume, tone and body language right. Focus on how you feel about something, rather than making a definitive judgement about it.

Avoid bestowing a lecture on children. Before you can expect your child to listen, you need to ensure you really listen to them. Children can be banal and repetitive on occasion and so all parents zone out sometimes, but if your child is feeling ignored or deprioritised, they are obviously way more likely to scream, whine or attention-seek. So give a child your full attention and empathise with their nonsensical ramblings about *Dork Diaries*.

If you find yourself losing it over the same kind of things each day – another wet towel casually discarded, a tormented sibling, a minor outbreak of arson – then ensure, as tricky as it may be sometimes, you maintain a strict focus on the positive. Always do your utmost to praise all signs of progress and compliance with warmth and enthusiasm.

Use a star chart to motivate your child for daily tasks such as keeping rooms tidy, brushing teeth and preparing things for school. Email us and we'll send you one. Is that very boring?

Likelihood of this wish delivering happiness should it manifest: Pretty strong. A home free of stress, as far as it's possible to achieve, is best for children and adults alike.

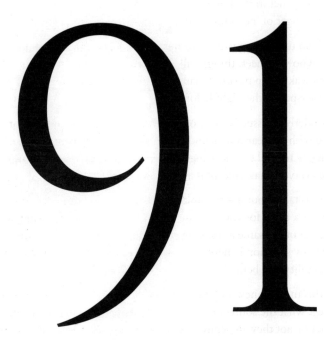

91

'I WISH I WAS BETTER AT
RELATIONSHIPS'

Here's why you suck at relationships. Maybe. You're so scared of being 'found out', discovered wanting and summarily rejected that you get in there first and mess things up, either through being distant and emotionally inaccessible yourself, or by engineering an event so dramatic there's no real coming back from it, like hooking up with some other random dude, just as things were starting to go well.

You pass off the demise of yet another nascent relationship as an example of your commitment phobia, explain to your friends that while the person they met in the pub last weekend might have 'seemed nice', they were in danger of 'becoming clingy' and how you need 'your space'.

There's an underlying issue here and ignoring it means that it doesn't matter who you meet, things will always mess up, even if you found yourself waking up next to Channing Tatum one morning after a bender in Wetherspoons the night before.

That underlying issue is a fear of abandonment and the best way of dealing with the fear is to acknowledge it's there. On some level, it's completely natural to fear being left; it's a primal fear that to some degree everyone has. Accept it and don't hate yourself.

It helps to talk about it – to explain to the object of your affection that this fear is a thing for you and you might need some help getting over it. That's not the same as making your issue someone else's; rather, it's that any situation benefits from the person at the heart of it taking responsibility and being honest.

With this more honest and self-aware platform in place, it is way easier to detect what the source of these feelings might be and decide rationally whether or not they are legitimate. Plenty of relations splinter over issues that only exist in the heads of the people involved – jealousy being one of the most common. Don't let yours be one of them.

Get in touch and we'll send you something to help.

Likelihood of this wish delivering happiness should it manifest: Pretty good. Alternatively, none of this is even faintly relevant to you and you just haven't met someone with whom you properly connect yet. In which case, we're sorry for droning on like a problem page from the kind of magazine you flick through out of desperation while waiting to have root-canal treatment.

92

'I WISH THE TERMS "FAT" AND "SKINNY" DID NOT EXIST'

Sadly, they do and always will. It would be unrealistic and naive to think we're ever going to live in a strange, sanitised world with a blanket ban on pejorative terms.

What's maybe more depressing is that very frequently these aren't words used by some weird controlling boyfriend or a jealous rival, but by women themselves about their own bodies – in fact, a disturbing number of women confess to having 35, 50 or even 100 hateful thoughts about their own shapes each day.

According to various pieces of recently published research, almost ten million women in the UK report they 'feel depressed' because of the way they look, girls as young as five are worrying about their size and appearance, and a quarter of seven-year-old girls have tried to lose weight at least once. Thousands of people a month google 'Am I ugly?' and half of British girls now admit they don't feel comfortable leaving the house without make-up on.

Elsewhere, 90,000 teenage girls undergo cosmetic surgery every year in Brazil while 85 per cent of girls in Hong Kong said they wanted to weigh less, despite only 5 per cent being clinically overweight.

The deification of size-zero models, the extraordinary rise of airbrushing and memes like 'thinspiration', 'thigh gap', 'beach ready' and 'pro-ana' are all symptomatic of the problem, which has at its foundation social media and the constant and limitless opportunities that exist to comment on the appearance of others. Increasingly, teenage validation comes from likes and comments, which typically tend towards the harsh; frequently shockingly so.

Body confidence doesn't come from trying to achieve the perfect body; it comes from embracing the one you already have. But you knew that already; assimilating it into your unconscious mind is the secret. Reiterative visual reminders can help with that, so email us and we'll send you a sticker to put on your mirror. It reads 'Caution: Reflections in this mirror may be distorted by societal stereotypes about beauty'.

Likelihood of this wish delivering happiness should it manifest: Pretty good. Alarmingly, the absence of self-esteem is a condition that is linked to poor academic performance, pre-disposition towards drug and alcohol abuse, self-harm and social isolation.

93

'I WISH I WAS FAMOUS'

Really, though? Wouldn't it be awful? When people talk about the upsides of fame they always seem to cite 'getting good tables in restaurants' and thereafter the list of benefits seems slightly to run out of steam. Let's instead look at the more obvious downsides.

There are numerous examples to support John Updike's belief that 'Celebrity is a mask that eats into the face', and if ever anything was going to distort your sense of identity and self-worth, it's fame. From the stars who insist no one makes eye contact with them, to those who send private jets halfway around the world to pick up some missing shoes, it's clear that fame, to express it mildly, tends to warp the values of those on whom it settles its momentary gaze.

Frequently fame goes further still and seems to revel in sending its subjects completely mad. Kanye West, for example. Shia LaBeouf. Tom Cruise. Britney Spears. Mel Gibson. Lindsay Lohan. Actually almost everyone famous, come to think of it. The best you can hope to escape with is some mild depression, with even Justin Bieber – who seems far from the most self-aware individual in the world – admitting he actually struggles with isolation, misery and betrayal because of his fame.

Fame takes away freedom and privacy. It makes it impossible to trust and increases the risk of harm to loved ones. Fame is also completely arbitrary. It's a hackneyed point to make, but fame isn't even discriminating enough to demand genuine talent. Fame doesn't mind who it descends on, safe in the knowledge that a few months hence, having driven its subject to the edge of the abyss, it can move capriciously on, happy to fleetingly alight elsewhere.

Ultimately fame is very happy to destroy those who possess it and has gleefully claimed hundreds of victims. Fame feels no guilt and the possession of authentic genius offers no protection against its ruinous influence.

On the face of it, fame sounds like a truly malignant force to be avoided at all costs. Yet we pursue it relentlessly, doing almost anything to attract it, and clinging desperately to it when it arrives.

Get in touch and we'll send you a copy of Lily Allen's 'The Fear' via iTunes; a highly perceptive and excoriating song about the true nature of fame.

Likelihood of this wish delivering happiness should it manifest: Poor. The downsides of fame are significant, i.e. it seems to make you a dick. Maybe in the future, as someone once speculated, everyone will be born a public figure and the rich will pay to remain anonymous.

94

'I WISH I COULD GET MY MOJO BACK'

Mojo is vital. It's what gives us energy, optimism, self-belief and creativity. It is infectious and persuasive and it makes it way easier to achieve our goals.

But sometimes it vanishes. Or at least slinks off for a week or two, leaving us lacking dynamism and faith in our own abilities. This happens to us all – everyone reaches a point sometimes where they lack direction and have zero energy to get back on track.

The loss of mojo is different to a proper depression – it's usually temporary and doesn't really carry the social stigma that many who endure more long-term issues feel accompanies them. It can be triggered by a specific event – frequently, the loss of a job or the demise of a relationship.

In the same way, it can be overcome reasonably swiftly, but may require concentrated focus. The key to regaining mojo is to never feel sorry for yourself and to draw strength from your ability to overcome obstacles: as Molière once said, 'The greater the obstacle, the more glory in overcoming it.' Self-pity and mojo cannot live alongside each other. So stop whining and moping around like a loser. Seriously, it's not sexy.

For you to return to your former sunny and upbeat self, you need to cast aside any thoughts of how unjustly the world has treated you, how you didn't expect your life to turn out like this, how things might have been different if only you'd been promoted or met the right person or been hugged more as a child or whatever. Focus on the now and move from there. Don't try and disguise whatever eventuality has robbed you of your mojo; just smile and say something self-deprecating like, 'My girlfriend has finished with me because I'm useless in bed'. Everyone will laugh and you'll immediately feel a bit better.

If you'd like a talismanic gift to help you regain your *joie de vivre*, then, as always, just email us.

Likelihood of this wish delivering happiness should it manifest: Face it, no one likes to see someone feeling sorry for themselves, so get out there and start bossing it again.

95

'I WISH I COULD GET A NANDO'S BLACK CARD'

Nando's is a phenomenon. The chain has over 300 restaurants around the UK and is the dining option of choice for premiership footballers, hip-hop stars, most of the former members of One Direction, the cast of *EastEnders*, Rihanna, Britney Spears, Lewis Hamilton and even Prince Harry. That said, Nando's is completely democratic and down to earth: their food is pretty healthy, consistently tasty and you can get out for less than a tenner a head.

Whenever referring to Nando's, it is very important to call it 'A cheeky Nando's'. Don't ask us why.

Their Black Card – or 'High Five' card as it's sometimes known – is something of an urban legend.

Apparently, it allows the cardholder to take up to five people out for a completely free meal in any Nando's at any time. The card has allegedly been sent out to numerous celebrities, including David Beckham, Ricky Gervais, Pixie Lott and Ed Sheeran.

Nando's themselves kind of refuse to confirm or deny the card's existence, saying only, 'All we can tell you for certain is that no one who's requested a card, no matter how politely, has ever received one.'

Despite their slightly coy response, we can confirm the Black Card is a real thing, rather than a myth in the style of the alligators in New York's sewers or the famous actor and the gerbil. The card exists, but as the company have already made clear, it's one of those celebrity perks that always seem a bit unjust, like the gifting suites brands lay on before the Oscars. If you've already been disproportionately rewarded with fame, riches and adulation, do you really need some free chicken as well?

That said, Nando's also offer a 20 per cent discount to police, fire service, ambulance service and NHS staff, so their priorities can't be completely out of whack.

Anyway, if you're not famous, you're not getting one. Sorry. Email us and we'll send you something else to cheer you up. Maybe some of the peri-peri sauce for which they are famed.

Likelihood of this wish delivering happiness should it manifest: Medium. Or maybe lemon and herb. God, we're funny.

96

'I WISH PEOPLE WITH SUBSTANCE ABUSE ISSUES WEREN'T SO STIGMATISED'

Scientific study seems to support the perspective that addiction is a treatable illness. Not everybody believes this, but it is now a commonly held point of view. If that is the case and addicts are essentially people living with a disease, then those who care about them and society at large are not going to progress very far if addiction is stigmatised.

Stigma is a reaction of fear, ignorance and prejudice; a negative attitude imposed on people by those who scornfully believe that addicts deviate from the norm and should somehow be separated from 'functioning' society.

Most addicts are parents, workmates, sisters and brothers. They hold down jobs, have friends, enjoy their weekends, value their relationships and go to social functions. They are, shocking though it may seem to some, nice people, very often self-medicating due to childhood trauma or other hidden demons. That's not to say all addicts are completely charming, but nor are all non-addicts.

Addiction is way too sophisticated and ubiquitous to be stigmatised: it does not discriminate between rich and poor, young and old. Now more than ever, cocaine, cannabis, alcohol, prescription drugs and even, increasingly, heroin are likely to be addictions of the aspirant middle classes. The reality is that most addicts are not hiding out in dingy squats, shooting up with contaminated needles, or resorting to crime to feed their habits. Some are, but they are a small minority.

Demonising addicts doesn't help anybody. In fact, it exacerbates the kind of clandestine behaviour for which addicts are frequently vilified, and makes it more difficult for them to access potentially life-saving treatment and therapy.

If you're worried you're an addict, or love someone who you think might be, then email us and we'll send something talismanic to keep you or them strong, as well as some suggestions for overcoming stigma.

Likelihood of this wish delivering happiness should it manifest: Pretty high. Addicts are people from every walk of life, who, successfully or otherwise, are usually trying their hardest to battle their illness: a battle way harder than most non-addicts will ever have to face.

97

'I WISH FOR THE PERFECT NEW YORK WEEKEND'

If you can, stay at the Nomad Hotel, or the Smyth Tribeca, or Aloft up in Harlem. Or Ludlow House. Or the Crosby Street Hotel. Or the Ace.

Friday night, get a reservation for cocktails at BlackTail, a new cocktail bar down in Battery Park. You can eat there too and the Rabbit Cuban Sandwich is amazing.

The following morning, take a stroll along the High Line, then have brunch at Bubby's. The 'Jalapeño Scramble Biscuit Sandwich' is the thing to order.

Then visit the incredible Armory on Park Avenue – the home of outsider art and cutting-edge creativity. There's nowhere like it on earth.

If you start to feel peckish, then grab a chocolate chip walnut cookie from Levain Bakery at 167 West 74th St. They're the city's best.

Then take a trip on the ferry to freaky Coney Island, wander around the cloisters at the Met Museum or take a cable car to Roosevelt Island and explore the spooky abandoned smallpox hospital.

That night, try and get to the Moth readings if they're happening while you are there, or check out some of the city's best improvised comedy at Asssscat 3000. No, that isn't a typo. For dinner share a roast chicken at Kingside or a cheeseburger at Minetta Tavern or Pop Burger.

Next day, do not miss the completely fascinating Irish and Jewish memorials in Battery Park. Then check out the *New York Earth Room* and the *Broken Kilometre* installations down in Soho.

At lunchtime go for sushi at 15 East in Union Square. Too healthy? Eat suckling pig at Cannibal instead or stroll across the Brooklyn Bridge and eat at the incredible Frankies 457 Spuntino.

Afterwards, wander around the hipster districts of Bed-Stuy and Bushwick, home to amazing galleries and one-off shops. Or shop at Fort Greene flea market at Bishop Loughlin Memorial High School (Saturdays, April to November). As the sun goes down, have a cocktail at the Westlight at the William Vale hotel and see if you can get a dinner reservation at Olmstead.

If you're planning a trip to NYC, then let us know. We'll create a bespoke itinerary just for you, tailored towards the kind of things you like doing.

Likelihood of this wish delivering happiness should it manifest: For a weekend, there is no better place in the world to wander the streets with your lover.

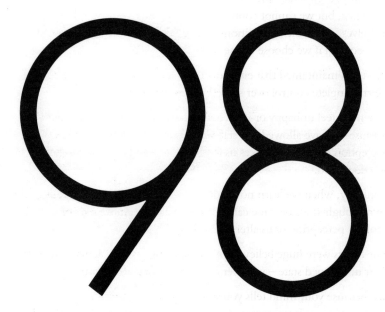

98

'I WISH I COULD HAVE PEACE OF MIND'

The ancient Stoics (Seneca, Epictetus and Marcus Aurelius, those dudes) believed 'Men are disturbed not by events but by their opinion about events'.

In other words, our emotions are dictated by our beliefs or interpretations of the world. Those beliefs are frequently inaccurate, irrational or self-destructive, but we have held onto them for so long they have become an intrinsic part of us.

The Stoics put all of life into two categories: the things we can control and the things we can't. We can't control other people, the weather, the economy, even what others think of us. Those things we can try and influence, but we cannot control. The only thing we have control over is ourselves: our habits, our actions and our thoughts. Even then, we only have control if we choose to use it.

Epictetus maintained that emotional problems arise when we try to exert complete control over something external.

When we feel unhappy or inadequate in some way this is frequently because we have allowed our self-worth to rest on other people's perception of us. This makes us feel powerless and uptight, anxious and depressed.

Ironically, when we learn not to do this and just focus on controlling our own thoughts, we become calmer, more peaceful, more likeable – and people's perception of us alters accordingly.

The Stoics were huge believers in seeing things as they actually are – in their unadorned state – whether or not it is palatable to you.

Just because your mind tells you something is a disaster or disadvantageous in some way doesn't mean you have to agree. We all decide what stories to tell ourselves.

The bottom line is this: no one is going to save you, so set about your problems with energy, creativity and indefatigability, for ultimately they are yours alone.

If you think you need some serious Stoicism in your life, then email us. We'll send you – in modern language, rather than ancient – their philosophy in a nutshell to pin up somewhere.

Likelihood of this wish delivering happiness should it manifest: High. It's rare to find someone, outside of Bhutan, who has achieved perfect peace of mind, but it's undoubtedly an aspiration for which it's worth striving.

99

'I WISH FOR A SURPRISE'

Totally.

Everyone loves surprises (although that's not actually true – 60 per cent of women hate them, according to research).

Anyway, email us and we'll surprise you.

Likelihood of this wish delivering happiness should it manifest: Hopefully high, but you'll have to see.

THE STORY OF CROWDWISH

People often ask about the kind of things that Crowdwish does, so here's a very swift look at some of them. The specifics of many of the actions remain confidential as they stray into pretty personal territory much of the time.

I think the first wish that came to the top of the list was 'I wish I could take a decent photograph' so I arranged for the person in question – a teenager at art college – to meet up with a portrait photographer for a cup of coffee. I think it went OK. I got a nice email from her afterwards anyway.

The next one I can remember was a wish that Amazon should pay corporation tax, so I wrote a sarcastic letter to Jeff Bezos asking him to close Amazon down immediately. Strangely, I never heard back from him. I guess he's still thinking about it.

Then people wished they could be better at public speaking, so I organised some one-to-one tuitions with this guy I knew who was the behind-the-scenes mastermind of the successful London 2012 Olympics bid, widely considered the fiercest competitive pitch of all time. That was great.

Then a butcher from Scotland called Wayne wished he knew more about his family history, so I arranged a consultation with the former executive producer of the genealogy show *Who Do You Think You Are?* – he is the godfather to one of my daughters and a pretty helpful guy. He got his team to put together a detailed report into Wayne's family going back generations.

Then people wished they were better cooks, so I organised for two people to spend the day in the kitchen of Racine, a multi award-winning restaurant owned by this amazing chef called Henry Harris. They seemed to like it.

Next, there was a wish around gender inequality in the workplace – specifically for women to be paid as much as men – so I wrote to the chief executives of the UK's hundred biggest companies respectfully suggesting that they audit their pay structures, with the aim of ensuring that their businesses were not the ones culpable for the discrepancies in pay.

Then people wanted a slice of the best pie in the world, so we reviewed some of the best pies in history, then had a load hand-delivered to people in places everywhere, from Indiana to New York to London. That was cool.

One time, people wished they 'could properly relax', so I contacted the makers of the 'Headspace' app and had them give me a load of codes so people could download it for free.

Then I had a wish come to the top of the list that related to a little girl who needed a bone marrow transplant so I produced and printed up posters and sent them out to 200 of the largest schools in the country to help find a donor.

The next wish was 'to have a cup of tea with Sir David Attenborough', the world's favourite natural history broadcaster. Fair enough. Who wouldn't want to do that? No one is who. I found the address pretty easily, then set off for Sir David's house. It's really nice without being too Abramovich-y and is in a prosperous but un-showy suburb of south-west London. In the front garden a herd of tiny elephants grazed. Not really. Sadly, the great man wasn't in but his charming daughter Susan was, so I talked with her for a bit. She explained that he was abroad but gave us some signed stuff. This is quite a typical Crowdwish thing and I guess important to understand: we absolutely do not guarantee to make the wish 'come true' – we just devote twenty-four hours to taking some action. The outcome may fall short of the objective sometimes, but we're strangely relaxed about that.

Then people wished they could dance without looking stupid, so I sorted out some guest-list passes for a thing called 'Morning Gloryville', which is a pre-work rave/exercise class where everyone goes crazy at 7 a.m.

Then there was a thing about cheering up friends, so we sent a little surprise to everyone who asked. Then there was the wish that the annoying columnist/commentator/opinion-on-a-stick Katie Hopkins could be served with a gagging order, so I worked out where she was going to be that night and posed as an autograph hunter outside the venue. I asked her to sign the bottom of a piece of folded-over paper that had a tongue-in-cheek gagging order written at the top of it. That went over pretty well on Twitter, back when Twitter was a thing.

A few times, people have made a wish along the lines of 'I wish that people would stop and help just one homeless person today with a blanket or drink', so on numerous occasions I have gone out and distributed food, sleeping bags and little packs containing things that I guessed – in a cosseted middle-class kind of way – might be useful if you live on the streets.

One time a mother in New York – on the run from some kind of abusive, maniacal, psychotic ex-husband-type – put a wish on the site about being unable to get help so I helped out with furnishing an emergency apartment as all her children were sleeping on the floor and her whole building had bugs. Then other Crowdwish followers donated duvets and sheets and so on. This again is quite typical of the dynamic – people wanting to help out others, even if they've never met them and never will. Without wanting to overstate the significance of this, it's life-affirming when it happens.

Then people wished that those who work for the NHS could get a nice surprise, so I took some flowers, donuts and cakes and things to a few hospitals around London. That's happened half-a-dozen times.

Lots of the wishes are more focused on self-esteem, feeling happier in one's own skin, more confident and so on. So I've sent out hundreds and hundreds of parcels of make-up, clothes, artworks and affirming jewellery (little silver discs on which are embossed positive statements), and I've set up a few consultations with stylists.

After someone wished they could write a novel, I arranged for them to sit down with an established novelist to get a better understanding of what it actually takes. Someone else had made progress but had writer's block, so I sent them a copy of Stephen King's *On Writing*, a box of pencils and some strong coffee.

On another occasion, a guy called Craig wished he could be Batman. I explained that sadly he couldn't actually be Batman, as Batman was a fictional character created by Bob Kane and Bill Finger. After the initial crushing disappointment, Craig reluctantly accepted this unwelcome news. I called my (lovely) former boss, who is now something really important at Warner Bros, and she sorted out this super-rare comic book for the guy, and I found a shooting script from *The Dark Knight Rises*, signed by Tom Hardy.

The same person at Warners has kindly sorted out tickets to premieres, which is also quite a popular wish.

The following week, the most popular wish was 'I wish I could make my own clothes', so I arranged an evening sewing class, hosted by someone who saw the wish on the site and sweetly offered to help out. We had pizza and wine and made some indeterminate, misshapen garb.

When the most popular wish was for the media to focus more on the good things that happen in the world, I made a faux-marble sign lampooning the *Daily Mail*, dressed up as a workman and fixed it to the side of their building in Kensington. It stayed there for an hour before they realised. You can still find it online if you search 'Crowdwish' and 'Daily Mail'.

When the wish was 'I wish we could remember those who died on AirAsia Flight 8501', a terrible aviation disaster in Borneo in 2015, I typed the names of each of the passengers who lost their life that day and put them in a sealed bottle one afternoon, which I then placed in the River Thames with a little note.

Another time, people wanted the government to stop the badger cull, so I dressed up as a badger and went to the Houses of Parliament with a funny sign in a hapless one-man protest. That's online too.

Over Easter weekend, after people wished for a nice surprise for the elderly, my girlfriend and I took 750 daffodils, 40 tulips and 27 Easter eggs to a residential home in Cumbria and helped the staff to arrange the flowers in their large day-room. The residents seemed happy, if a little confused.

Wishes relating to the older generation are quite common. After she was mugged, I replaced a pensioner's handbag, its contents and £100 cash, after people wished that older people were treated with more respect.

A guy made a wish that he had his own theme tune, so a friend who's a DJ spent a day in a studio composing one for him. It was actually super-catchy and I can still hear it in my head ('Mike, yeah, he's amazing. Mike, yeah, he's fantastic', etc.).

Quite a few wishes are for more kindness in the world, so when those come up I always do some kind of 'random act of kindness', as they're called, slightly nauseatingly. One time there was a really sweet old couple in the supermarket near my father's house, so I paid for their shopping. Their trolley contained a large Easter egg, some nice flowers, a few bottles of wine, lots of groceries and some boring but necessary cleaning products.

Often the wishes are political or express dissatisfaction with the people who are meant to be in charge. One time the wish was 'that farmers got paid a fair price for growing our cheap bananas', so I left a box of bananas and a sarcastic note at the constituency office of Vince Cable, who was Secretary of State for Business at the time.

In a similar vein, I sent Ed Miliband a map of his constituency after people wished that MPs spent more time with the voters they were meant to represent. I delivered to Jeremy Corbyn two very nice shirts and ties after people complained he was too scruffy (thanks to Nick Wheeler, who owns Charles Tyrwhitt shirts, for those). I swear I've seen Corbyn wearing them at PMQs but I may be wrong. Another time I sent George Osborne a tampon in a luxury box as a protest against the tax on feminine hygiene products.

I produced and gave away posters for people to put in their windows to discourage UKIP canvassers. They were pretty popular. Then I sent a glitter bomb to a far-right leader (google 'Ship your enemies glitter' if you don't know what I'm on about). Another time, I wrote to Donald Trump asking him why he said all those disturbing 'locker room' things.

A couple of times, the wish has been quite a blunt monetary thing – 'I wish for a Topshop gift card' or 'I wish for £100' or whatever – so sometimes I've done treasure hunts for people to find cash or vouchers in phone boxes.

Another time, I sent a cake to Stephen Fry in lieu of the knighthood that people wished he'd been granted. He was typically gracious in his acceptance.

After people wished that the Nigerian government did more to help the schoolgirls kidnapped by Boko Haram, I left 180 Post-it notes on the door of the Nigerian High Commission, each bearing the name of a missing girl.

I also changed the signage at the Iranian Embassy so that the welcome one highlighted their terrible human rights record. But a scary voice came over the intercom so I ran away quite quickly.

OK, to accelerate slightly, as a result of wishes made I have raised the money for a disabled girl to get a specially adapted trike, provided funeral flowers for a young man, helped people get over break-ups, sent a dog some mince pies, left flowers at the Israeli Embassy, given out warm hats and gloves to those living on the streets, sent sensory toys to children living with autism, given away make-up, iPhone chargers, Christmas decorations, Maca powder, bedding, hot water bottles, interior design books, healthy snacks, peace charms, anti-racism stickers and sewing equipment, organised a competition for budding psychics, left a tree to be planted in a rundown area, laid flowers at a memorial to those killed in the Paris attacks of 13 November 2015, helped a left-handed child feel more confident, given away prints and T-shirts to those living with ME, visited those living alone, helped people thank those to whom they owed a debt of gratitude, made and sent out some anti-bullying stickers, offered discounts on iPhones and MacBooks, helped people travel the world by paying for tickets, sent out dozens of cleansing lotions for people worried about their skin, distributed signs telling people to clear up after their dogs, set people up on blind dates, sent people on training courses to get a better work/ life balance, helped someone get closer to her dream of sending her boyfriend's ashes to their final resting place in the Sahara Desert, rewritten people's CVs for them, delivered hamburgers to someone's office as a lunchtime surprise, paid for someone to have a decent haircut, sent a care package to the migrant camp in Calais, changed the signage on the London Underground after people wished that their fellow passengers would smile more, helped people renting flats who were being abused by their landlords, provided discounted personal training, helped people with anxiety issues, sent out teeth-whitening powder to those who felt self-conscious about their smiles, left lottery tickets all over London, bought a guy in South Africa a ticket to see Russell Brand, provided a flight to see the Northern Lights, arranged a special offer on a yoga retreat, sent someone called Gabby a very cool, waterproof HD camera, helped people set up their own websites, paid for someone to have a one-night honeymoon, created bumper stickers to encourage safer driving, left flowers and chocolates anonymously outside the flat of an elderly person who lived alone, visited a beautiful twelve-year-old dog called Bella who lives with her homeless owner on the street in central London and took her a variety of treats and some dog food, helped with college tuition fees, arranged for someone to have a backstage tour of the Royal Ballet in London, helped make a back garden safe for someone living with a severe disability, distributed care packages to those living with chronic pain, sent out books to help people with depression, donated food to homeless shelters and food-banks, sent someone a kit for the perfect day off, including a bottle of good red wine, some upscale muscle soak for a relaxing bath, two novels, a DVD featuring Manchester United's best ever goals and some chocolates, offered entertainment at an old people's home, sent out a herbal sleeping remedy to dozens of insomniacs, paid for a little girl called Lily to have two riding lessons, helped acknowledge a bunch of amazing volunteers, got someone a pass to Disney World Florida, helped someone meet a Beatle, sent a cinema voucher and a bunch of sweets to take with them, dispatched Stoic philosophy, mailed those who asked a poster of Caitlyn Jenner, sent a little boy called Tommy a bunch of *Star Wars* toys, mailed feminist badges to those who requested them, sent someone's parents fifty handwritten cards to thank them for all they had done for her, organised a personal finance seminar, aided children with dyslexia, helped out an impatient father, mailed people portable ashtrays, given away tickets to Secret Garden Party, helped a little boy see the sea for the first time, left daffodils around the place for people to find and take home to their loved ones, arranged for someone to hug a baby elephant, given away tickets for the finale of *The Voice* in the United States, handed out umbrellas in the rain, given away beautiful temporary tattoos, helped a very sick boy called Denver receive an amazing number of birthday cards, sent someone flowers to boost their confidence after a difficult period, offered to de-clutter someone's house, left a cheeky sign in Harrods taking a stance against condescending women on make-up counters, paid for two weeks car hire so someone could enjoy a road trip, sent someone called Pete a Polaroid picture autographed by Eddie Vedder of Pearl Jam, and dozens of other things that you're now too tired to read about.

This all sounds a bit immodest and 'I did this, I did that, blah blah blah'. It sincerely isn't intended to read like that and the site has done hundreds of things that have not been broadcast in any way. I'm only spelling it out here as, like I said, the question is often asked and I'm trying to spare you going online and reading loads of old blog posts.

The Crowdwish project is ongoing, and one wish every twenty-four hours still gets actioned, as it has done for over 1,100 days.

You can download the app from the app store, visit the site at www. crowdwish.com and see the archive of wishes at blog.crowdwish.com/ archive.

Peace Out.

So many debts of gratitude owed; firstly, to my fantastic editors at Constable, Andreas Campomar and Claire Chesser, without whose enthusiasm and support this book would have retained the status of most books (a hypothetical notion, much discussed but never produced), to my agent Rachel Mills at Furniss Lawton/James Grant who has been completely amazing and has a fetching undercut, to Liane-Louise Smith at James Grant and Alexandra Cliff at Peters Fraser + Dunlop for sorting the foreign rights, to the supremely helpful Howard Watson for his brilliant copy-editing skills, to Sean Garrehy and Chris Harman for their truly incredible job on the cover art, to Bianca London for her redistribution of the spoils, to Kathy Marr for her conscientiousness, diligence and kindness in all things, to Julia Parker for her intelligent and thoughtful suggestions, to Phil Roberts for his unflagging enthusiasm for the project as a whole and genius input on the TV concept, to Al Edgington at Conde Nast in Los Angeles for believing in the show and doing everything in his power to make it happen, to Ben Bilboul for hosting me unquestioningly and never asking what I was still doing in his office after all that time, to Kathyrn Coster and the many hundreds of people who have supported the Crowdwish project online from the earliest incarnation, to my father whose love and support are always unfailing, to his special friend Judith who privately opined that this book was headed 'straight to the bargain bin' (so, dear reader, if that's where you've just fished it out from, Jude was totally right, so well done), to my beautiful daughters for being so understanding on the innumerable occasions that I was boringly preoccupied at my laptop when I should have been giving them my full attention, and to my amazing girlfriend Wu-Tang – 'I only wanna see the light that shines behind your eyes'.